Lest We Forget

SU3A Memories of WW2

Edited by

Helen Collingwood, Irene Davy,
Dot Sutcliffe

ISBN: 978-0-9553938-5-3

First published in 2011

Cover design by Iris Associates, Sheffield

Printed in Great Britain by
The Print & Design Factory Ltd, Sheffield

Acknowledgements

We would like to thank all the contributors who shared their stories with us and made this book possible, and also Peter Hughes and Denise West for their work in the early stages of the project, and Shelagh Woolliscroft for her support.

Thanks also to Iris Associates for their cover design, and the printers, Print & Design Factory.

We are deeply grateful for financial help from the Memories of Work Group and Sheffield U3A.

The photograph of the Sheffield Blitz on the front cover is courtesy of Sheffield Newspapers Ltd.

Foreword

In my role as Chairman of SU3A at the start of our Silver Jubilee Year, it gives me huge pleasure to welcome you to this collection of captivating stories about World War Two, which cover a wide variety of experiences.

I would like to congratulate all the members who have worked so hard on this collection of memories, and also those members who were prepared to relive their experiences in the presence of a stranger. Whilst some enjoyed the process, for others it must have been very painful. I thank them all for taking part.

The result is a 'first' for Sheffield U3A and I hope it will inspire members to consider similar projects. I also hope that teachers will see the book as an important resource and that they will invite U3A members into schools to tell their stories – stories that none of us should ever forget.

Shelagh Woolliscroft
Chairman of SU3A 2009-2011

Introduction

The seed of this project was sown in 2009 when a small group of members with war-time experience were interviewed by Year 10 students at Tapton School. At the same time, the SU3A Executive Committee was looking for a shared project to mark our Silver Jubilee Year of 2011.

Also around this time, talk turned to the passing of Harry Patch, the last surviving veteran of the First World War, who had played such an important role in communicating his first-hand experience of war to the younger generation. Someone raised the point that we are now reaching the stage where the generation that lived through the Second World War is beginning to pass away, and that, for the benefit of future generations, it is vital to record their stories now.

As a result, one SU3A member, Peter Hughes, took a lead role in setting out to collect and record for posterity other members' Second World War stories. Initially Peter advertised in the SU3A's Links magazine and then held a meeting of interested individuals. Some members wrote their own accounts, while others were interviewed and had their stories written up. A small group gathered alongside Peter to collect and edit the stories with a view to publishing a book of members' memories. Sadly Peter had to pull out of the project late in 2010 due to ill-health, leaving three stalwarts –

Irene Davy, Dot Sutcliffe and Helen Collingwood - to carry on. It was decided to publish the book in time for SU3A's Jubilee Day celebrations on 30th June 2011 at Wortley Hall. We wish to acknowledge our gratitude to Peter, whose vision and enthusiasm provided the impetus to complete this book.

Many books about World War Two have already been written. However, as this particular collection of memories illustrates, each individual person experiences events in a way unique to them. The following collection of stories shows how ordinary people's lives are turned upside down by war and how they cope and survive the sometimes horrific experiences that war brings. Members of SU3A come from a diverse range of backgrounds and this book includes the experiences of people from many different areas of this country and beyond, including Holocaust survivors and those living in enemy countries during the War.

Happily, enough of the older generation are still around to give us an idea of life in the armed services, but the majority of contributors were children in wartime, and the vividness of their memories shows what an impact war had upon their lives. In some cases the whole future direction of a family or individual was changed. An extract from one participant's diary juxtaposes the mundane everyday aspects of life with some of the horrors of war to great effect.

We found the process of editing this book an interesting, enlightening and moving experience. We hope that our readers find it an enjoyable read.

The Editors

Contents

On the Home Front

The Second World War was the first one to fully impact the civilian population of this country in a way that previous wars never did. Many people who stayed at home found themselves subject to similar perils to those faced by the armed forces, and some of them lived daily with the prospect of death and destruction.

Many of these stories are from people who were children or teenagers during the war, and their memories are vivid. For some, the noise of fireworks or the sound of an air raid siren still has power to cause a shudder. Others, living in, or evacuated to, areas not in the firing line, freely admit to having had an enjoyable time.

The stories in this section cover three main themes: first, the Sheffield Blitz, second the wartime experiences of Londoners, and third, the many aspects of 'ordinary' life during wartime, which to those who did not live through it, seem anything but ordinary.

The Sheffield Blitz - December 12th and 15th 1940

*During the first night of bombing, **Dorothy Freeman's family** had the added strain of being located in three different places, so until morning came, each of them had no idea whether the others had survived – and what a morning it was!*

Dorothy Freeman

Who could forget the Prime Minister's words on the 3rd September 1939? I was sixteen at the time, living with my parents and sisters at Hunter's Bar, Sheffield, when over the radio I heard him announce – "This country is now at war with Germany."

I remember vividly the night of the Sheffield Blitz. It was the 12th December 1940 and I was 16-years-old. I had a crush on a boy called Horace and his mother had invited me round to their home in Nether Edge. What I didn't know was that she had also invited his girlfriend so it was definitely a case of "three's a crowd". Suddenly, a bomb hit the house next door. It was such a shock. There had been no warning sirens and for a moment we all looked around wondering what it was. But not for long. The living room curtains were on fire and Horace's mother and I rushed to put them out. He stood with his mouth open. The next few hours were hellish and we spent them sitting on the cellar steps. There were six of us in all as we had been joined there by his "nutty" aunt and her nurse.

Meanwhile, my father who was in the Home Guard, was stationed up on the moors and watched in horror from a great vantage point as Sheffield burned. In the early hours of the morning his platoon came back to Sheffield. He hurried to our home and when he found I was out he rushed to find me. He told me the journey was a nightmare skirting around bomb craters, carnage everywhere. He eventually found Horace's house on Priory Road and sweating, filthy and anxious knocked on the door. I opened it, and just like he had been invited to a posh tea party I said, "Do come in." He didn't half kid me about it for years afterwards.

We walked back through the craters and I reached home. It was almost breakfast time and my sister and I were due to go into town to work. None of the trams were running and there was no bus service, so we walked into town. Many of the overhead tramlines had been brought down. My sister worked at Walsh's Store in High Street, where we stood and watched in horror as Walsh's was still burning and almost totally destroyed.

I will always remember the Sheffield Blitz for it was the day I realised my first love was not the hero I imagined – my Dad was. So, I left Horace to the girlfriend and soon I met Dennis. He was in the R.A.F. and one day I had been to visit him in York. Train journeys were very hazardous during the War as German bomber planes would follow the train lines and target them or the stations. As I arrived back in Sheffield there was an air raid on and the station was blacked out. It was so dark everywhere. The street lighting was non-existent because of the risk of air raids. Normal street lights were covered, allowing only a small amount of light on to the footpath. However, I decided the best thing to do was to start walking towards home. I picked my way up Howard Street and gradually made my way into town. Suddenly there was a plane above me and someone shouted "Quick, get down". I laid full length on the pavement as the bomber swooped down Surrey Street, spraying bullets as it screamed overhead. It was petrifying but I was lucky and unhurt and brushing myself down carried on for home.

For years you could see the bullet-holes in the masonry of the City Hall. Over the years to come I would often pass them by, remembering that night. Then a couple of years ago, during the refurbishment, they disappeared and another scar has gone and now is probably only remembered by me.

Another family in a similar position was that of ***Bessie Renwick****, who spent the night away from home in the cellars of the YWCA (Young Women's Christian Association) in Division Street.*

Bessie Renwick

In 1939 I was nearly 19, living with my parents in Fulwood. There were just the three of us at home, as my older brothers and sisters had already left. I was working for the Council in the Transport Department offices. I had hoped to be a teacher, but my father was invalided out of his job and so my parents could not afford the training – they needed me to get a job and earn some money.

On the night of the first Sheffield Blitz, which was a Thursday, I had gone into town to attend a class at the YWCA on Division Street. The sirens went at 7p.m. and we all went into the cellar, where we stayed until 4a.m., sitting on benches or boxes, with nothing to do except listen to the noise of the planes and guns. Worst of all was the whistling sound the bombs made as they came down, and the fear of wondering where this one would drop. It was very frightening.

When we came out in the morning and walked towards Barker's Pool, the city was one huge mass of flames. It was a sight I'll never forget. As there were no trams or buses, I had to walk the four miles home. All along the way glass was dropping out of windows, masonry falling down, and the contents of shops were strewn all over the road. Halfway home I was turned back because of an unexploded bomb, so I had to find another way, eventually arriving home at 7 a.m. - it had taken me three hours to get there. My parents were waiting on the doorstep, they didn't know till that moment whether I was dead or alive, and were tremendously relieved. The next Blitz was on the Sunday night following and I was at home, so we spent the night in our Anderson shelter.

Beryl Harrison*, in her teens and already out to work, experienced not only the bombing, but, like Bessie and Dorothy, the destruction wrought in the city centre as she walked to town next day.*

Beryl Harrison

Three weeks after the outbreak of the Second World War on 3rd September, 1939, I celebrated my fifteenth birthday. A blackout was imposed at the beginning of the War and ARP wardens patrolled every night to make sure that no houses had lights showing. We all had to have blackout curtains. We lived on Folds Crescent at Beauchief. My father, having joined the Fire Spotting Service, would don tin hat and venture out into the darkness to see that all was well. But, on 12th December, 1940, all was not well. By then we were used to air raid warnings, searchlights and barrage balloons. We heard enemy aircraft flying over regularly with their distinctive droning sound and then, of course, the sirens would go every time.

On 12th December my father came home as usual at 5.40pm and told us to get into the shelter straight away as he could already see bombs falling. It was a brilliant moonlight night, almost like day. A minute or two later the air raid warning went and the incendiaries started to fall near us. We had an Anderson shelter at the top of the garden. They were intended to hold seven people. Within a short time there were 13 of us as the neighbours rushed to take cover where they could. An incendiary bomb fell on the bungalow across the road from our house and another on the road on the other side of the house beyond the top of the garden. That one landed on a gas pipe and started a fire which the ARP men rushed to put out. Then the heavy bombs started to fall and the noise they made as they exploded and the noise from the anti-aircraft guns as they opened up was deafening. My father now took charge. He had served in the Royal Artillery for 21 years and had been in the last War. When we heard bombs whistling down he told us to bend over and put our heads between our knees. This was to protect against bomb blast and falling shrapnel. By the time the All Clear sirens went at about 4:30am we had been in the shelter for 11 hours.

The East End steelworks survived unscathed but not the town centre or the suburbs. [I now understand from some people who have studied the subject that they believe it was never the intention to have the steelworks put out of action, as Hitler's long-term plan would have been to have his headquarters at Chatsworth and to keep the steelworks intact for his own use. The raid on Sheffield was intended to break our morale.] The next morning we listened to Lord Haw Haw, (the British traitor), on the radio: "Garmony calling, Garmony calling, Garmony calling, (that is how he spoke). Hello Sheffield, you caught it last night, didn't you? You thought that we could not find you. Do you know how we did? We followed the flashes from your trams". I remember so well, this was what he said. Maps of where the bombs fell which were published much later after the War showed that the bombs had in fact fallen on the Abbeydale tram route into town and had fanned out in all directions too, of course.

My sister, then aged 19, had joined the WAAF a month after war was declared. Her first uniform in those early days had consisted of a raincoat and beret, plus gas mask in a carrying case and a kitbag. She was home on a week's leave so was with us when we had the Thursday night Blitz. The next day she realised that she must have her uniform for when she returned to her station and she had left it to be altered at a shop on Chapel Walk in town. We set off together to try to get it back. At the tramstop no trams appeared so we set off walking. We walked through to Millhouses but when we got to Abbeydale we began to see bomb damage. At one point near the Abbeydale Cinema there was an enormous crater, burnt-out trams and damaged housing. We were forced to go by the back streets and regain the main road further on.

From then on it was one horrific sight after another as we reached the town. From the beginning of the Moor onwards there was almost complete devastation with burnt-out trams and buses, some still blazing. Many shops and other buildings were in ruins and the roads impassable. Men who were there dealing with the situation asked us what we thought we were doing. When we explained our reason for coming into town they grudgingly let us proceed, telling us to take great care. We reached Chapel Walk at last. There were two blackened bodies lying by the wall on the left hand side as we walked down. At last we reached the shop to find it undamaged and to our relief the tailor was there. He had battled his way into work, like many others, and the uniform was ready and waiting to be collected. We now had to walk all the way home to Beauchief. We were exhausted, but we were young and soon recovered. Joan went back to her station in Nottinghamshire the next day in her uniform. On the Sunday night we had another heavy raid but nothing like as bad as the Blitz on the 12th.

Audrey Morris *was not quite three-years-old during the Blitz, yet she says she can still see clearly in her mind's eye, the scene when their shelter door was blown off.*

However, for Audrey, the horrors of that night were quite eclipsed (at least at the time), by the sudden acquisition of an early Christmas present.

Audrey Morris

We lived in a small back-to-back house in Pearl Street in the Sharrow district of Sheffield. It had one living room/kitchen, a bedroom and an attic, with a privy across the yard. I can't say that I remember much about the house, just vague recollections of going to buy sweets at the local shop, but then I was only two years old. My third birthday was to be on the 21st of that month.

My real memories begin just before that when the siren sounded, warning of an air raid, and my mother and father and I with our neighbours crammed into the concrete shelter in the yard. There was a loud explosion and the door was blown off, knocking my father out and he fell onto my mother. I could see through the opening the row of houses with all their windows shattered and the night sky blazing fiery red. I can still see that scene if I close my eyes.

It was decided that we should all go to a bigger shelter a fairly short walk away, near Cemetery Road, but first my father had to collect something from the house. We went back into the ruined building and, while I waited at the bottom of the stairs with my mother, my father scrambled up the slope of rubble that was all that was left of a staircase. He reappeared a little later, slipping and sliding and clutching something rather large and covered in dust which he put down beside me saying "Father Christmas has been early this year." My big round eyes saw the biggest doll's pram I had ever seen and a beautiful doll with golden curls and eyes that closed when you laid her down and a pretty pink dress. I was picked up and put in the pram (yes it was big enough for me) the doll was put in my arms and our little group proceeded through the blazing streets to the next shelter.

I felt like a princess and could only feel the joy of having the doll in my arms and none of the horrors of being bombed out, that all came later, but just for a while it was magical. I can still hear the crunch of broken glass and the feel of it under the pram wheels as we went down the steps into the air-raid shelter, where I was welcomed royally and given a drink of water from a large stoneware barrel and there was warmth and singing to pass the night away.

We emerged next morning into the cold, grey mist of a December day, into a barely recognisable place with piles of smoking rubble where there had been houses. We were homeless and had to live for a time in the one room that my grandmother rented from her niece and which was only lit by a gas mantle.

I gradually became aware of the austerity of wartime Britain but I kept my pram and the doll that I called Betty and I was the envy of my friends because of them. I have no idea where my parents managed to buy such pre-war luxuries. They must have cost them a lot of hard-earned money but they were, obviously, not going to let Hitler's bombs stop me having them.

Ivy Beaumont, *nearly five-years-old, was living near the East End steelworks, and recalls the night her home was seriously damaged. Her older brothers and sisters had been evacuated to the country, and Ivy notes how changed they were when they returned, because their lives had been so different. Many evacuated children and their families must have experienced the same.*

Ivy Beaumont (nee Goldsmith)

I was four-years-old when the War began, living at 40, Makin Road, Attercliffe, near Brown Bayley's Steelworks, with my parents, three sisters and one brother. My sisters and brother were all evacuated to East Leake, but I was not thought old enough to go, so on the night of the Sheffield Blitz I was at home with my parents. It was two days before my fifth birthday. Before the Blitz my father worked very long hours in the steelworks, and sometimes he would push me up Prince of Wales Road in a pram, to escape the bombing, as it was the steelworks they were aiming for.

The first Blitz took place on 12th December. In the shelter were my parents, our next door neighbours and Blind Joe, who had been blinded in the First World War. We were at the back of the shelter, Joe was in the corner and I was sitting next to Betty Johnson, the girl next door. The bombing went on all night, non-stop.

Betty had her arm round me when a big landmine fell on Bridport Road, and our shelter was lifted right up out of the ground. The windows, the door and one side of our house roof was also blown off. That landmine destroyed St Alban's Church, Coleridge Road, and killed about 39 people in a big shelter nearby. The wardens said that the blast had blown all their clothes off. The people who lived near the canal, and therefore nearer the mine than us, could not return to their homes at all because they had been rendered unsafe.

On Sunday night they came again, to Brown Bayley's. As we had no shelter, we went down the cellar steps. There was no tarpaulin for our roof at first and so the rain and snow came in. The windows were boarded up for ages and we all lived in the small downstairs back room until someone came and covered the roof with a tarpaulin.

During the War my mother often went to visit my brother and sisters in East Leake. Two of them were at the village blacksmith's, one at the barber's and one at the gardener's house. Mr James told my mother he knew the bombers were heading for Sheffield as he saw them fly overhead. When my brother and sisters came back from evacuation, they had all changed, because of the different lives they had lived.

I still cannot bear fireworks to this day. As soon as the bangs start, I cower, and I never go out those nights.

Vera Wibberley *was living near the city centre – an area badly hit by bombing, and her home was totally destroyed.*

Vera Wibberley

Thursday night, 12th December 1940, was the first part of the Sheffield Blitz, the second attack being Sunday the 15th. We were living in Lancing Road at that time, near Shoreham Street. At 7 o'clock the sirens sounded and we all went down into the reinforced cellar (we did have an Anderson shelter but my father wouldn't let us use it as he didn't think it was safe).

Living near the city centre, there were a lot of bombs falling in our area - we were near to Laver's Woodyard which caught fire early on and the flames lit up the sky. The houses across the street and also next door were badly hit and our own house nearly demolished with the blast, also our Anderson shelter in the back garden was flattened, so if we had been in it we would have been killed.

I can still remember the choking dust around us and the terrifying noise as we crouched in the cellar. My father was on the cellar steps above us and I remember my mother looking up at him and screaming. She thought there was blood pouring down his face, but it was beetroot juice from a glass jar of beetroot on the pantry shelf above which had fallen and smashed on his head and given him concussion!

After we had pulled ourselves together we crawled through the tunnel into next door's cellar (all the houses had this tunnel leading from one house to the next right down the road in anticipation of an emergency like this), and struggled out of the rubble three doors down the road on to the pavement. Looking up, we saw German planes in the bright red sky, swooping down over the rooftops and machine-gunning us. My father threw me down in the road with himself on top of me. My mother was in a passageway nearby. The bullets were flying around us but miraculously none of them hit us. When things quietened down a bit, we got up cautiously and ran down the road to my grandma's house and into her cellar, where we stayed for the rest of the night, and also for the next month as we had nowhere else to go. In fact six people spent Christmas in that cellar!

The next day we went back up the road to see what was left of our house, which was very little. The staircase was left, and we saw that my wardrobe had fallen across my bed, throwing all the blackened bedding on to a tree nearby. The mirror inside the wardrobe door had smashed into all my clothes, and everything was black with dirt and, of course, unwearable.

Across the road a friend of ours had been killed by the blast. Because all the mortuaries were full, she had been left on the pavement, covered by a tarpaulin, for three days and people were stepping over her until she could be moved.

A few days later we went back to the house again to see if anything could be salvaged. The Army were there making the area safe. My father had some bottles of home-made wine in the cellar which had miraculously survived and he gave the soldiers these bottles. I can see them now, all sitting on the pile of rubble and drinking from these bottles!

We could not save anything at all from the debris – all our furniture was ruined, together with all our clothes. We had a lovely piano and I was having lessons, but we never got another one. The compensation we eventually received covered merely basic items of furniture such as beds, tables, chairs, etc. We eventually got a house to rent in Charlotte Road next to my grandma's house, which was nothing short of a miracle as there were no houses to be had after the Blitz, and from there we had to make a completely fresh start.

Another house was later built on the site of our old house in Lancing Road, but a few years ago there was another scare as an unexploded bomb was found on the site, which was fortunately rendered harmless, so someone else had a lucky escape too!

*Nine-year-old **Muriel Jackson**, living on the Wybourn estate, also lost her home completely, but after some months of living with relatives, her family was lucky to get a house at Southey, in which she still lives. Muriel has also written a poem expressing her feelings about her old home, which is included at the end of this account.*

Muriel Jackson nee Hobson

I was born in 1931, and was 9½ in December 1940 when the Blitz came to Sheffield. I lived with my parents and older brother George (born 1921) in a new council house on Maltravers Terrace, Wybourn. My father, who had been out of work for some time before the War, had a job in the steelworks making munitions. Our house was semi-detached with a big garden, and my dad had dug a hole and erected an Anderson shelter there, which we shared with our next-door neighbours.

I had a siren suit, and an identical one for my baby doll, who always came to the shelter with me. The night of the Blitz my dad and brother came home from work and we had our meal. When the sirens went off we went down into the shelter, but my brother insisted on staying outside, at the top of the kitchen steps, "watching the fireworks" as he put it. My father was furious with him. Suddenly we heard a hammering on the shelter and my brother said there had been a big bang next door, and he thought he had got some broken glass in his hair.

When the All Clear sounded, George went off to see if his girlfriend, Betty, was all right and when we went into our house, my mother said "we are lucky". The only thing that was broken was a glass sugar bowl on the table and a lot of soot had come down the chimney. The man next door came to see my dad and said "will you come and look at my porch – there's a big hole in it". My father said "I don't like the look of that" and went off to get help.

The first man he brought back, an Air Raid Warden, said it was too dark to see, so dad went again and brought back someone from the Home Guard, who said "I'm not happy about that Mr Hobson, I think it's a time bomb – get your coats on and take your families down to the school". We had just arrived at the school when they said “Mr Hobson and Mr Holiday, your houses have just gone”. My mother collapsed and had to be revived with sal volatile by a lady across the road.

Very little was salvaged from the ruins, except luckily a few old family photos and a few possessions my mother valued and which she had kept in a box in the shelter. Later neighbours told us they had seen some children across the road wearing my clothes, which had been stored in an old tin trunk, but mother did not go back to argue – she was too upset.

My uncle lived at Grimesthorpe, and our two families had agreed that if one of them was bombed out, we would live together, so we went to stay with them. Three nights later, on a Sunday, the bombers came again, and this time it was Grimesthorpe and the East End steelworks that were hit, but not my uncle’s house. We were in the cellar, which had been reinforced and had bunk beds in it.

We stayed there several months, and several times a week my mother went to the Town Hall to see if our friendly rent collector was in. One day she saw him, and he said he did miss calling at our house and the cups of tea she gave him. She asked for another house and eventually he said “I’ve got the keys for you, for a house on Southey Crescent”. This was exactly where my brother had always wanted to live and we moved there in March.

When Mum got the keys, my godmother went with her to see the house. It was also semi-detached. We were given a wooden table and four chairs, a wooden bed for my parents and a table shelter (Morrison shelter) to go in the front room, and a few cups, saucers and glasses. We were also given some blankets, made of brown wool, and the label on them said - 'This is a present from Australia for British courage'.

When we definitely knew we were leaving, Mum went to Grimesthorpe School to say I would be leaving and along I went with her to our new house. Later in the day she sent me to the bus stop to look out for Dad and show him where we lived. When he and my brother got home from work, they went through the 'for sale' adverts in The Star and came back with a lovely sideboard and matching table. My dad stained the chairs we'd been given which were very basic. He also painted, varnished and grained the top of the Morrison shelter which he and mum usually slept in. She used to polish it each week. When my friend Joyce came to stay in the summer holidays, mum would put dusters on our feet and let us dance about on the table top to polish it. Joyce thought this was wonderful.

A Room from my Childhood by Muriel Jackson

The room I remember when I was small
A grandfather clock leading off from the hall,
A warming pan hanging – polished handle up higher,
Ready to be filled with hot coals from the fire.
Cushions aplenty upon the old couch –
How I remember the house – but then such!
It all tumbled down in the Blitz of 1940.
But I remember it well as a child for it
Taught me – that nothing in life is sure or
Forever –
Except the love that I felt in that house
Leaves me never.

Kathleen Hebdon *was living at* Frecheville *well to the South of Sheffield, but her area did not escape unscathed, and on top of that, she was suffering from measles!*

Kathleen Hebdon

Our house was newly built at 30 Burbage Grove, Frecheville when I was born there. With a struggle the house had been furnished and the garden set out with well-made concrete pathways.

Impending raids of German bombers had spurred the three or four families around us to build a large communal air raid shelter, from railway sleepers. This was dug deep into the soil at the bottom of our garden path and covered by soil to deflect the worst of the shock of an explosion.

My Father worked in the East End on vital steel work necessary for war, and was exempt from call up. However, this meant that all the men were in defence organisations, in his case the Home Guard. In his great coat, which did valiant service, tin helmet and his rifle he was away all hours when not at work.

Air raid warnings would see our very nervous mother literally 'drag' my older sister and myself to the shelter. After the Thursday raid, although telephones were very rare, a 'bush telegraph' story went round about the severity of the damage and loss of life. My Mother worried so much about the safety of our aged grandparents at Heeley that my Father, taking my sister with him, struggled to get to them. They passed all the devastation in the city centre and duly found the old folk safe in their house.

On Sunday 15th December I was suffering very badly with measles (no antibiotics then) and it was planned that in order to prevent the other four children from being infected, my mother and I should shelter beneath a tent-like arrangement made from the-three piece suite. However a very caring neighbour would not go along with this and came and made us go in the shelter - the children would have to take “pot luck" with the infection.

The bombers were supposed to be heading for the East End Works. However, they were heavily defended with search lights, balloon barrages and Ack Ack guns and as the men took their last quick drag on their Woodbines they heard the plane turn and head for home, dropping its bombs on our suburb. The first bomb fell close by and immediately the second blast blew the men into the shelter. When all went quiet, they ventured out to find a huge crater where the garden had been and the houses shattered. My Father was strangely consoled by the fact the concrete of his path had withstood unscathed the worst Hitler could do.

The three piece suite was at the far end of the room from its position near the crater and we would have perished for certain. The furniture was rescued and stored in the local community centre. The piano looked okay but under the lid it was found to be filled with rubble. The paltry compensation was based on pre-war prices but wartime prices bore no relation to these! Franklin's did a roaring trade in restoration. None of our belongings were stolen from their storage. The twins, Tony and Pat next door, found their budgerigar had perished in his cage but he was the only fatality that night. The kindly neighbours, Mr and Mrs Bower at number 28, took the two now homeless families in, and the 10 of us shared their small home for three months until re-housed elsewhere. The men-folk were out at all unsociable hours, with my father snatching a few 'winks' on top of the pile of clothes filling the bath, little chance of a bath in those days!

The first of the three bombs fell at the top of Linley Lane where the occupants were sheltering under the stairs. The gas main had been ruptured and the local policeman earned himself a bravery medal for going in and leading them to safety. The third bomb made a direct hit a short distance from our home on an air raid shelter. Rescuers dug frantically but were unable to find any sign of the occupants. Eventually someone ventured into the owner's home to find the couple sitting either side of the fireplace, shocked. They had never stirred and were safe.

***Margaret Walker**, whose home was in Crookes, remembers not only the Blitz, but the night later on in the war when Sheffield saw its only Doodlebug (V1 Rocket). She, like Vera, also recalls one of many incidents years after the War, when unexploded bombs were discovered.*

Margaret Walker

Our family was living in Tinker Lane, Crookes during the War. At 10 years of age I was digging to build the shelter in the garden, as a protection from the bombs. I suppose I helped in a small way. We had a small place with four seats for our family. Father gave us rubber to put between our teeth, and ear plugs.

They were soon needed, as a land mine screamed down around the area of Mulehouse Road. I didn't want to miss the excitement so I took the ear plug out of one ear! It was very close, but it was a 'dud' (unexploded) – just as well – I might have lost my ear drums.

Father was in the 1914-18 War, so he had lots of tips, such as how to fold the camp bed army-style, and put as many blankets underneath us as over, for warmth. He started the Local Defence Volunteers (LDV), later called the Home Guard, in our area, and trained the young men and older men who were not eligible to join up, in warfare. Radios were a speciality - they were taken up to Lodge Moor and an answering platoon was across the valley. He enjoyed it!

He was also on night watch during a raid. By this time our little shelter had extended to one with four bunks, a heater and a table for our homework. In the winter of 1940-41 German planes used to come over every night at 6 p.m. to wear us down, so all the people in Tinker Lane sat on the gate to wait, and when we heard the drone of the engines we would rush into the shelters. Our tea was ready there and hot water bottles, so there was no fear on our part.

We slept in the dugout nightly for almost a year. [I once gave a talk on the War to a class of 7-year-olds. One boy wrote "Margaret lived underground for a whole year!"]

The day of the Sheffield Blitz was on my Mother's birthday, December 12th 1940. We slept through it – never heard a thing. Then Dad went out on duty and came back shouting - "Get up. Sheffield has been bombed and Mrs Wright's shop has been hit". It was a tripe shop.

Because it was a school day, up we got and went in the car to Notre Dame School off West Street. The drive there was in and out of bricks and overturned cars, homes split in two, with beds hanging out of rooms, the clothes still on them. Many roads were cordoned off, so it took a long time to get to school. It did not occur to us that there would be no school! Out of 900 pupils, there were seven of us. On my suggestion we went up into the classrooms and swept up all the glass. There were no windows left in the school, and incendiary bombs had landed on the roof, which the caretaker put out. After we ate our lunch in the kitchen, we were sent home. That journey was a walk up steep hills, in and around bombed houses, and it also took a long time.

Dad had to go to the Rolling Mills at the steelworks to check the electrical work. The steel foundries were not hit, just the shopping centre and small houses around. We were dismayed at the bombing of the only cinema in town, the one where we used to go for tea upstairs for a treat. The other cinema was The Scala, which was taken over as a canteen for workers. I used to go for lunch, and Mother was serving meals in the Women's Voluntary Service (WVS). Another job she had was to serve tea to troops at the railway station. The great rush every time a train came in had to be prepared for.

Other recollections

I saw a Doodlebug (V1 Rocket) fly past our house on its way to Manchester over the mountains. We heard about the explosion next day. The normal range for these V weapons was only as far as London and the Home Counties, but occasionally a faulty one would get further.

Postscript

Roundabout 1980 I was working in Shoreham Street when a 16 foot land mine was discovered in a back garden. It had to be defused and lifted out by crane. The original Air Raid Wardens' report from 1940 said: "Three land mines came down. Two were found and defused".

The Londoners

Traumatic as the Blitz was for Sheffield and other provincial cities, London suffered the longest and most sustained periods of bombing. As attacks on the capital city had been expected, most children were evacuated to places of safety in the country at the start of the War in September 1939. However, when many months went by with no air raids, many families brought their children home – just in time to experience the full horrors of the Blitz.

Children whose homes were damaged or destroyed either returned to the country, or stayed in London with their parents, only to be evacuated again in 1944 when the V1 and V2 rockets began to fall.

Most of the stories in this section are from people who were quite young children during the War. They illustrate how incredibly fractured and nomadic were the lives of many London families for the best part of six years.

Jean Daniels *and her family were amongst the few who survived the horrific Balham Tube Disaster. After their home was destroyed, her whole family moved to the country and embarked upon a very different style of life*

Jean Daniels

I was born in Stepney, East London in 1934 and was five-years-old when the War began. I lived at home with my parents (who ran a jellied eel and pie shop) and my older brother (aged 11) and sister (aged 12). My sister attended the local Grammar School and I had just started at Nursery. We knew we were due to be evacuated but the Prime Minister of the time sent us away much too early, without giving our parents any warning. One day we went to school, had a label tied on us and were put on a train. Our mother thought we had just gone to school, so we didn't even have suitcases with us. We were taken to Hove, to a hall where people came to choose who they wanted. As my sister was at an age to be useful, she was chosen first and I went with her, but our poor brother still wet the bed so was not popular. He went to live with two spinster sisters who had him sleep on a camp bed in the hall.

It seemed we were there a long time but we weren't really and were soon moved to a Mrs Nye in Brighton. She was not a very nice person and took in lots of evacuees to make money. From Brighton we were moved briefly to Wraysbury in Surrey, where we were looked after by an old couple who had a garden full of soft fruits - we loved that. A plan was afoot to send children to safety in Canada, but my mother wouldn't let us go. That was just as well because the ship they were on was torpedoed and nearly all the children drowned. After that, the scheme was abandoned. My mother came to visit and took me home and while I was at home, war was declared. My parents were so busy with the shop that they hadn't much time to bother with me. When my sister was around she acted as my surrogate mother, something she later told me she bitterly resented.

Then the bombing began. We'd come home from school, pick up blankets and go to Balham Tube Station, to sleep in the Underground. We were there when it was hit by a landmine which also hit the water mains. My sister and I had just got back from the toilets when the bomb hit and we all heard a rushing sound. We thought it was a train coming to rescue us but it was rushing water from the fractured main. There were electronic gates at the entrance which were locked, but as our side of the platform was near them, my father managed to get us all over them, but everyone on the other platform was drowned.

As there was no electricity working, we had to walk up the escalators and emerged into the street with the Blitz still on. We were temporarily put up overnight in a reception centre in a hall somewhere, but when we got home in the morning it was to find that our house had been looted. I don't know what happened to the shop but dad got a van and loaded into it whatever was left of the furniture and drove us to Hayes in Middlesex, where we were initially accommodated in a Salvation Army Reception Centre. In those days there were lots of houses available to rent and we soon got one and moved in.

The War changed our lives as a family completely. Hayes was just a small country town in those days and a much better environment than the East End of London. The result was that our lives took a very different turn. I was seven when we moved to Hayes and at 21 I met my husband. He had lived round the corner from us in Stepney but had come to Hayes during the War as we had. Although I did not notice this till I got older, I think the War had more effect on me than the others. For one thing, the bomb had perforated both my ear drums, but despite all the inspections by school nurses, this fact was not discovered. By the time it was discovered I was too old for them to repair the damage, with the result that I have lost the hearing in my right ear completely. It also left me with an anxiety complex.

A few years ago I was at the cinema watching a war film, and suddenly onto the screen came Balham Tube Station and the episode of the bomb and the drowned people. I couldn't help it, I just shouted out "I was there", to the embarrassment of whoever was with me and the amazement of the people around us.

Sylvia Blindt's *family enjoyed life in the country so much that they did not return to London until 1952.*

Sylvia Blindt

I was six-years-old at the start of the War. We lived in Camberwell in London at that time. There were six children in our family but I was the only one at school. We were told that our school was going to be evacuated but we were not told where we going. When I told my mother she said that I wasn't going to go by myself so she came along with my three sisters.

One day all the children were given gas masks and we were told to meet at one of the big London stations. There were hundreds of children but not very many mothers. We ended up in Billingshurst in West Sussex. We went into the village hall where some of the village women were allocating children to homes. We were sent to a bungalow only to find that there was another family already living there which upset my mother. To my mother's horror, we realised that this family was infested with fleas. My Mum complained and they were moved out.

Despite the War, I had a lovely childhood. I went to the village school and loved it. School dinners cost three old pence but sometimes we'd take the money and buy bread and jam from the village shop to eat instead. We had a garden to play in with conker trees. I went mushrooming in the fields and picked primroses to sell to raise money for Dr Barnardo's. There was a blacksmith in the village and I can remember being completely enthralled watching him shoe the horses. At the weekend, my Dad and my brother would cycle the 49 miles from London to visit us.

One of my hobbies was collecting shrapnel. One day a German plane was shot down so my Dad took me to the site on the crossbar of his bike. He picked up a leather gauntlet which was lying on the ground only to discover that there was a hand in it. He quickly threw it away!

There were American and Canadian soldiers living in the camps in the area and they were very good to the local children. They gave us parties at Christmas, sweets and chewing gum. My mother used to invite them round for tea sometimes. We kept chickens so we were able to give them eggs for tea which was a bit of a treat as eggs were rationed. The soldiers smoked cigarettes called Sweet Caporal. The packets had pictures of planes on them. I collected the pictures and learned to identify the planes when they were flying over.

One of my brothers volunteered for the Army as soon as he was 18 and was sent to Burma where he was a stretcher-bearer. Once he sent us a parachute from which we made underclothes and blouses. Another brother was a Captain in the Army in Alexandria. My father was a master cabinet-maker and he was sent to Shoreham-by-Sea to work on building the landing craft for D-Day.

My mother owned a dress shop in London and one of my brothers was a stamp dealer, selling his stamps through her shop. A stamp collector in Ireland got in touch with us and was concerned that we were short of butter. He would post it to us, flattening it to send it through the post.

I can remember when ice cream first became available at the end of the War. I went to get some from the dairy about four miles away but by the time I got home it had melted and wasn't ice cream at all.

We liked our life in Billingshurst so much that we stayed until 1952.

Claudine Mears *was evacuated with her boarding school to the Lake District, and apart from a brief sojourn back home to celebrate VE day, she remained in the Lakes for two years after the War.*

Claudine Mears

I was four-years-old in 1939, and an only child. My mother was Swiss and my father English, and we lived in South London. Each year my mother and I would spend six weeks in the summer in Switzerland, but my father could only join us for two weeks, and then returned to his work in the Civil Service.

The result of this was that when it was clear that war would be declared, we had to get back to England quickly, or we would have been stuck in Switzerland for the whole of the War. It meant a long train journey through France, so soon to be occupied, and we made it back just 12 hours before the outbreak of war.

My father had fought in the trenches during the First World War and lost most of his toes with frostbite, so he could not join the armed forces. Instead he was sent to Harrogate to undertake top secret work, and we didn't see him for five years. We experienced some bombing in London, and had both an Anderson shelter in the garden and a double-height Morrison shelter in the downstairs bedroom.

My aunt taught in a boarding school at Weybridge, so I was sent there for safety, and my mother (whose English was not very good), worked in a factory for the entire War. This school was later evacuated to the Lake District and I remained there till I was twelve years old, i.e. two years after the ending of the war. Unfortunately my aunt had the idea it would be wrong to show me favouritism, and in consequence treated me with extra severity, only relaxing a bit if she took me out on our own. We called her 'the old vinegar bottle'.

I was ten when the War ended, and was sent home to Mum for a while, joining in the parties that celebrated the end of the War. Our party was held on Streatham Common; not in the street like most others. When my Dad came home he was a stranger to me, but he was a very good father.

Michael Blindt *lived in the London area throughout the War, and admits to over-indulging at a VJ Day party!*

Michael Blindt

I was five at the start of the War. We lived in Edgware which was thought to be a safe area so I wasn't evacuated and the rest of the family came to stay with us. There were people sleeping everywhere.

One night I was sleeping in the hall on a chair bed when a parachute mine was dropped. Fortunately it landed on the nearby railway embankment instead of directly hitting our house. It blew the front door in and I ended up wearing it round my neck. The ceilings fell down and the windows were blown in too. My sister was in her cot in the front room. The day after we found that her cot was full of glass but there wasn't a mark on her. We had a glass-fronted china cabinet in the room whose doors were always kept locked. The doors were blown open but only one pane of glass was cracked.

After that incident all the visitors left, deciding it wasn't safe after all.

We had an Anderson shelter in the garden but the clay soil meant that it was always full of water so we never used it.

My father was too old to go into the Army so he became an air raid warden. He was a professional violinist but he went to work at HMV repairing Spitfire radios. He wasn't good with his hands so we used to tease him by saying that his lack of expertise was probably helping the German cause instead of ours.

One day my brother was playing cricket in the Hendon area when his bails were blown off by a V2 rocket. He was declared "not out" and calmly continued his innings.

At one point during the War my mother had to go into hospital. My young sister and I were sent to stay with our grandmother in Chiswick. It was the time of the incendiary bomb raids and most nights we sat in the windowless hall of her flat singing the songs we knew like “Daisy, Daisy”, “When I Grow Too Old to Dream” and “She'll Be Coming Round the Mountain” until the All Clear siren went.

I remember walking past demolished streets on my way to school – streets that had been there the previous day.

On VE Day we had a big party in our street. There was a bonfire in the road which destroyed the tarmac. Later on VJ Day we had a party at school with lots of ice cream. I ate so much that I was sick when I got home. My mother wasn't pleased!

Adrian Padfield's *nomadic existence at least involved being evacuated to friends or relatives, initially with his mother. These episodes were interspersed with periods at home in London, until the next lot of bombing sent him back to the countryside.*

Adrian Padfield

I was born in Chiswick in February 1937 so I was only 2½ at the start of the War. Even so, I remember being evacuated in September 1939, with my mother, to her brother who lived in the country near Wolverley in Worcestershire. My uncle had a bungalow made from asbestos sheets enclosed within a wooden frame. He had a windmill in the garden to power a dynamo that charged 12 volt batteries for lighting only.

By Christmas 1939, we were back in Chiswick as London was still quiet – this was the time of the "phoney war" - but when the Blitz began in autumn 1940, I was evacuated again to family friends in Romiley, Cheshire. My abiding memory from this time is of being taken on a visit to a nearby signal box. I was handed up into the cab of a steam train and the driver blew the whistle. It terrified me and I can remember the fright it gave me to this day.

The following year I returned home to Chiswick and at 4½, started school. Walking there on my own one morning, I came across some soldiers drilling in the street and, fascinated, I stayed to watch them. Consequently, I was late for school and got into trouble for embarrassing my mother who was a teacher at the same school.

My father had built a shelter in the garden and for what seems like most nights in 1942, I slept there in a hammock. The shelter was damp and nasty as it was buried under the lawn. The hammock was my grandfather's, who was in the Royal Naval Air Service in WWI.

Towards the end of 1943, soon after my sister was born, a bomb was dropped at the end of our road. Luckily it missed our house. It was the only time I remember feeling really frightened.

In 1944 I returned to Wolverley with my mother and baby sister because London was then under attack by flying bombs (V1s). I used to play with a local farmer's son in the fields and woods near our homes. I can remember a field of reddish sand with yellow wires sticking out. They were detonating wires for explosives used to excavate under a hill. I discovered later that this was to construct an underground factory in a series of tunnels at Drakelow for the Rover car company, which at that time was making aircraft engines. One day in the woods I found some strips of silvery stuff, known as "window", which was used to reflect enemy radar beams over Germany. The woods had been used as a practice area for the dropping of this stuff. Further memories include going to Sunday school in my brand new coat and getting tar on it (in trouble again) and being given "candy" by American GIs who were stationed in the area.

In autumn 1944 I went to Romiley again and my mother and sister went back to Chiswick, where I returned in the New Year 1945 when I went back to school there.

My only memory of VE Day is of going to a big party in a house down the road. I remember being put to bed when it got late with the neighbour's daughter who was a year or two younger than me – and getting teased about it.

Pamela Bennett *left London after enduring nine months of nightly bombing, but was lucky enough to live with relatives – as it happens, in Sheffield.*

Pamela Bennett

I was almost six when War was declared. I was living in London with my parents and sister who was 20. We lived at the top of Shooters Hill overlooking the Thames. I could see St Paul's from my bedroom window if it was a clear day. Our house was on a line which enemy bombers took after crossing the Channel to reach London.

As we had a garden, we could have an Anderson Air Raid Shelter. These were corrugated metal. My Father had been in the Royal Horse Artillery in WW1 so he knew how to make the most of it. It was dug into the ground and Dad made it as watertight as he could and then put a wooden floor on top. I can remember carpets and then a double mattress and bedding. Mum put curtains around the metal walls and there was a paraffin heater which was on in the daytime.

Not much happened for about a year but then on 7th September 1940 I was at a party, probably a seventh birthday, when the Blitz began. My Mother came to take me home. I can remember seeing the Thames on fire and the smell wafting over the Thames of the sugar factory on fire.

There were barrage balloons and fighter planes during air raids so the noise was tremendous. We had a large crater in the road outside our house and the roof had been damaged when the bomb fell and we had tarpaulin on the roof. It was a good job that Mum and Dad had worked so hard to make the shelter safe and comfortable as we slept there for the best part of nine months.

I wasn't there all that time but I can remember it clearly. As soon as it was dark the air raid siren sounded, a noise I still don't like to hear, and we had to get into the shelter or dug out and stay there till the All Clear, usually next morning when it was light. We took down food and thermos flasks of hot water. I can remember playing cards. I think Dad fixed up a trailing light from the house but I am not sure. We got used to the planes and the bombs every night but the sound of low flying planes coming was not good. The noise was tremendous. This was every night. I went to school at all sorts of times depending on when the All Clear went. We all enjoyed looking for pieces of shrapnel on the way to school and working out where the bombs had dropped during the night. There were daytime bombs also but not too many. Mum said she could sleep reasonably well in the shelter knowing that if we were hit we would all die together.

After a few months my parents decided that I should be evacuated. All children had to leave London unless you had a garden to have an Anderson Shelter. Not all did go and some came back quite soon. I wasn't evacuated like most with a label around my neck. I came to Sheffield to stay with Mum's brother in Fulwood. I didn't know them very well but I soon did. As they hadn't any children at that time, they spoilt me tremendously. I went to Oakbrook School on Fulwood Road, played with a girl about my age who lived across the road and generally had a very nice time. After a year or so I went back to

London as the War wasn't so bad then. We must have been back in the house then and I went back to school as before. There were still delayed action bombs and life was not easy - especially for Mum queuing for food, looking after the chickens we had to have and preserving eggs. Dad had an allotment as well as the garden so we had plenty of vegetables.

I suppose about a year went by and the V1 bombs or Doodlebugs or buzz bombs began. They were awful as there was not much warning and they came in the day. While they were making a noise you were okay but if it stopped it just dropped from the sky and you had to dive for cover. There were 2500 of those. And then came the V2 rockets which were awful   No warning at all.

So, I was sent back to Sheffield. My school uniform didn't fit any more so I went to Nether Green School. I can remember being very happy there. There were some 'proper' evacuees there, also from London and sometimes we were told to "go home". I only stayed for a few months and went back home again.

When it was all over, we went into the centre of London and everyone was so happy – it's a day I won't forget. I can clearly remember VE Day and VJ Day when we had street parties.

Pat Donoghue *was also evacuated to the city which has now become his home, but not until he had experienced some traumatic events.*

Pat Donoghue

In 1939 I was three-years-old, living in New Southgate, London, with my parents and two sisters. We lived in an old Victorian house, three storeys high. We had the bottom two floors and the top floor was empty. At the back of our house was a railway embankment with very wide tracks beyond it.

One night in 1941 my mother had decided not to go to the shelter during the air raid, so we got under the dining table. Father was out fire watching. A landmine fell nearby and the top storey of the house collapsed onto the second floor which collapsed onto us. We were trapped under the rubble. I recall being lifted out through a window.

After this my sisters and I were evacuated to Wales, a village called Pontrhydfen, near Aberystwyth. The lady of the house was a real Welsh dragon. She didn't want us and her children didn't want us either. Friday night was bath night, in a tin tub brought into the kitchen. After she had washed our hair, she would get a big can of cold water and throw it over us to rinse it. We walked four to five miles each day to school throughout the winter and we were so hungry we tried to dig up vegetables from the fields, but the ground was frozen solid. The kids at school all spoke Welsh, but we knew they were talking about us and taking the Mickey. Their chant in English was "Evacuees, all got fleas".

We went back to London, this time living in Forest Hill. I was evacuated to Northampton for a time, but I've no idea how long. The only memory I have of it is that the man of the house tried to teach me boxing. Back to Forest Hill again and by 1943 we were so used to hearing the sirens that we tended to ignore them, thinking "It can't happen to us". Some happenings at that time were when 26 Fokker 190 dive bombers came over, flying at treetop level. One machine-gunned a young mother and her baby in New Cross High Street. Then they all circled round Sandhurst Road School and dive-bombed the playground at lunchtime, killing 23 children and six or eight teachers. The pilot later boasted on Paris radio that the bombs fell exactly where he wanted them to.

That was not my school but on the same day I was coming home from school, walking uphill with my two sisters behind me. They had just met the mother of one of their friends. I heard a roar, looked back, and saw that they had vanished. Six planes flew up the road, firing at me. Later we could see a cannon hole in the wall of one of the houses. These were part of the same pack that killed the schoolchildren and the mother and baby. My dad told me off for running away. He said I should have either run towards the plane or laid down flat.

Then in 1944 the Doodlebugs (V1 rockets) came. We were in our Anderson shelter near the house, when a Doodlebug dropped in the road 60-70 yards away. It blew the shelter door off, and I saw a pair of my sister's knickers flying through the air. My most vivid memory is the dust.

So, we were evacuated again, and this time my mother went with us. We came to Beighton, which was then in Derbyshire. No-one seemed to want me and I went to two or three places before I was accepted. After the War I'd come back in the holidays to stay with the family I'd been billeted with. I remember they used a local meeting hall as our school dining room, and as I was the only one who liked cheese flan, I got everyone's portions. Here I stayed almost till VE Day.

My memory of VE day is of the wonderful street party. The chef from one of the big London hotels lived on our road and he made a huge, magnificent cake. I never knew where they got all that food from after years of rationing; it was such a marvellous spread. I also remember VJ day, August 1945, because I was in hospital having my tonsils out and they wouldn't even let me go onto the balcony to watch the bonfires.

*A new wave of evacuees left London in 1944, with the arrival of the Doodlebugs (V1 Rockets), and quite a number of them came to Sheffield, which was considered to be beyond the range of the rockets. Whilst on holiday some years ago, one of the editors of this book met **Brenda Whitaker**, who belongs to a South London U3A. Brenda said what happy memories she had of her time here after her home in London was severely damaged. To this she added an invitation to stay with her on a visit, saying "I shall feel I have paid my debt to Sheffield." This is her story.*

Brenda Whitaker

On a sunny afternoon in June 1944 I was 12-years-old when a Doodlebug (V1) fell on a house a few doors away from my home in Tooting, South London. Another had fallen a road or so away earlier in the day and my father was attempting to carry out simple repairs to some glass windows at the rear of the house. My mother was at work.

Sadly, one of our neighbours and a passing cyclist were both killed. Also the second V1 clearly did more damage to my home so it really was barely habitable for us all. I was able to stay with my friend, Joy, who lived nearby. Her brother nobly gave up his place sleeping under their table shelter. My parents managed, with difficulty, to stay in our damaged house.

In the 1914-18 War my father had served in the 9th Royal Lancers and a few days after our house was damaged, a retired officer of the regiment called to offer us a share in his home in Wimbledon. I moved there with my parents. How fortunate that I was then able to leave Joy's home and comforting shelter, for it meant that her brother could retrieve his place under the table. A few days later, after Joy had been sent to stay with relatives outside London, the house suffered a direct hit from a V1. Her parents and brother were saved by the shelter and were able to be dug out, shaken and dusty, but unharmed.

After I had stayed in Wimbledon for a few weeks, my pregnant sister Olive joined us, as she in turn, with her

RAF husband, had been bombed out of their flat in Brixton. Clearly we were overcrowding the kind officer in Wimbledon. Doodlebugs continued to fall and our house was still uninhabitable, so as another friend called Sylvia had been evacuated to Sheffield, it was decided that I should join her. The parent of another evacuee who had also moved there said she would arrange to find a billet for me.

She found Ada and William Clark, who lived at 53, Far Lane, Hillsborough, who agreed to have me. How very kind they were, and welcoming without being overwhelming. Looking back, I realise how lucky I was. The Clarks had no children and must have been in their late 40s or early 50s. They gave no sign of dismay at having a near-teenager dumped on them. Maybe in my possible insensitivity I was not aware of any unease. Will Clark worked at a cutlery factory. Even now I remember the logo it used. It was the figure of an eye (a common logo I believe). He was a quiet man and did not talk about his work, but did proudly show me the knives and scissors he had made.

Ada Clark came originally from the Channel Islands – she was a gentle soul and sometimes not in good health. I think perhaps she or her family had had a shop. She had retained some of the stock. She remembered that certain items were in short supply in the First World War e.g. combs, soap and stationery. Going into the room where she kept them was like going into an Aladdin's cave. She was generous too, and would sometimes give me an item from Aladdin's cave for my own use. She had strong

Christian beliefs. As a result I was not allowed to knit or make anything on Sunday. I could read (perhaps one of her fascinating 1930s magazines like Home Journal) or write letters.

With frequent letters from my parents and sister (no telephones of course), I do not recall being particularly homesick. I am sure this would be due in a greater part to the welcoming and normal atmosphere of the Clark home, as well as having my friend Sylvia nearby. In September Sylvia and I went to the local Central School. I had attended Grammar School in London, but I do not think there was one nearby.

The Clarks introduced me to their friends, a friendly shopkeeper (in Hillsborough Lane perhaps), and neighbours. To this day I can recognise Grieg's Piano Concerto that was played by a young woman who lived next door. That same young woman would take me on Sunday evenings with her friends to a nearby chapel, where I joined in singing hymns with gusto. I have pondered over the years why I sometimes chose to take myself off to a nearby Church of England on a Sunday morning. I was not particularly religious, so I wonder if it was my attempt to make clear that I was still my own person.

On a Thursday afternoon Mrs Clark would run a small crafts class. I cannot remember the exact title, but it was something like 'Ladies' Shining Hour' and was, I think, linked with a church group. A young woman called Eileen Dyson would come with the others. With them I learned to make leather purses by thonging pieces together. I also twisted small pieces of gold or silver-coloured metal strips into an eight shape. I would then link each piece together, attach a green or gold glass drop, and there I had a necklace.

What else do I remember about my happy time in Sheffield? Learning to play croquet in the garden at no.53; walking round Sheffield centre, seeing the factories and learning that the smell I noticed was the smell of hops; taking a shining copper jug to the door to be filled by a milkman from his jug; learning what a dolly was and how to use it when washing clothes. Then there were the bus rides to see the lovely areas around Sheffield.

In November my home in Tooting had been repaired so it was habitable. I was pleased to see my father who came by train to take me home but sorry to say goodbye to the Clarks. I went home carrying necklaces that I had made for my mother and sister, plus a leather purse. I was pleased to be there for the arrival of my nephew Alan in late December. V2s (rockets) began arriving in January.

For a while I kept in touch with the Clarks by letter, but then I learned from Eileen that Mrs Clark had died. I did not keep in touch after that. I was sorry, for I shall always be grateful for their kindness and the period of normality they gave me after what had been a traumatic time.

Daily Life in Wartime

This collection of memories illustrates just how extraordinary (to those of us who never lived through it), is the juxtaposition between the ordinary events of daily life, and the totally different conditions imposed by war, especially when seen through the eyes of children. The contributors in this section lived in various parts of the country and whilst some of their experiences have much in common, they could also differ greatly.

Pat Roddis *remained in Sheffield for most of the War. She recalls gas masks, fund-raising efforts, and an unusual Christmas Eve in an air-raid shelter. Happily for her, that wonderful character Father Christmas, managed to locate her even there.*

Pat Roddis

I wasn't evacuated for most of the War but stayed in Sheffield where I went to Ecclesall School. We had to have air raid practices and practise wearing our gas masks which were horrible. At home we had a table shelter which was like a big metal cage to sleep in. It took up the whole of the front room. We also used the cellar as a shelter and there was a trap door in the dining room which we had to climb through to get into it. My Dad dug it out deeper which resulted in a pile of earth outside the kitchen window. He propped the roof up with wooden supports and installed bunk beds for my brother and me.

My Mother had to sleep in a chair when we were down there. It was a cold, miserable place.

It's surprising how clear some of my memories are. I can remember my Mother saying, "don't go outside without your gas mask". I was in the Brownies and one day I forgot to take my gas mask with me to the Brownie meeting. Brown Owl made me go all the way back home to get it.

The standard-issue gas mask cases were made from cardboard and not very attractive. A new gas mask case became a popular present – I had a black patent one.

We spent a lot of our time raising money for various charities: the Catholic Women's League, who raised money to build huts, canteens and hostels for the forces; Aid to Russia and Aid to China. I received a letter from Clementine Churchill (Winston Churchill's wife) who was the chairman of the Aid to Russia Fund, thanking me for "the trouble you have taken to help brave Russians in their struggle and in the glorious defence of their country".

To raise money we held garden parties in our garden where we sold the lavender bags and hairbands we'd made and the buns my Mother made. One year a friend came and did a conjuring show for us. We probably raised less than £10 in all the time we were doing it but it was quite a lot of money then and it kept us entertained. My Mother and I also made glitter wax flowers to sell while we listened to the radio in the evenings. They were made from this wax which we wound round twigs. We sold them for 1s and 6d a bunch which was quite expensive in those days. People used to order them in colours to match their living rooms.

I was evacuated at the height of the Blitz and went to stay with an Auntie in Scunthorpe. We spent Christmas Eve in an air raid shelter at the bottom of the garden. I was worried because I thought Father Christmas wouldn't know where I was. He did find us though and I got a doll called Angela. My Dad knew somebody who owned a fruit farm in North Wheatley near Doncaster so my Mother, brother and I went to stay there for a time. I thought it was heaven. There was an outside toilet with a wooden seat which had two big holes in it with a little one in the middle.

I had a brown siren suit which I loved. One day I went to school in it and on the way there I rolled in the snow drifts. When I got to school the teacher made me take it off because it was wet. I was very upset because there was another girl at school wearing one and she didn't have to take hers off.

On VE Day we had a big street party. We lived on a hill which meant that everything rolled down to the bottom end of the table. Unfortunately I was sitting at the top end! My Dad put a flag pole up in our garden and on VE Day he flew the Union Jack on it. We had another party on VJ Day. The Mothers saved up their rations to make sandwiches, jellies and cakes for the parties.

After the War, there were lots of Polish boys who had escaped from the Russians still living in this country. My Mother offered to have one of them to stay as she thought he would be a playmate for my eight-year-old brother. To my Mother's dismay when he arrived he was actually about 18. I was 14 so my friends and I had a wonderful time with him. He left after a couple of weeks and I heard nothing from him. I found out later that he had written to me but my Mother had not given me his letters. Many years afterwards my husband and I traced him through the Polish Airforce Association. He came to visit us in 1975 with his wife and sons. I was really glad to find out what had happened to him and to know that he was okay.

*Eight year old **Greta Phillips** lost relatives in the Sheffield Blitz, while her father and uncles served in the armed forces in various theatres of war.*

Greta Phillips

I remember my father's shop on Castle Street being bombed. I went with my father – there was just a big hole. The only thing left was the safe. My father took the frizzled money to the police station. He was then left without a job. He was called up for the Navy - I remember my mother being dressed in a voluminous white nightie, opening a letter to say that my Dad had been called up.

My aunt, uncle and three cousins were killed at Parson Cross by a land mine. The family had just moved into the house. I heard that, whilst the furniture was being moved in, my aunt had a premonition that something awful was going to happen there. Their eldest son was at a dance and got home to find his family gone. He joined the Navy and he is now 88.

When I was eight in 1940, I was chosen as May Queen at school – I was Lilac Queen. I still think that the reason I was made May Queen was because all the other kids at school had fathers who were in munitions factories, but my father was in the Navy.

Whenever my father came home on leave he would never go to the shelter in the garden. He and my mother never went in our shelter – we would go in our neighbours' shelter. How we got everyone in I don't know. I wouldn't go in the shelter till my white Persian cat Peggy, was in too. I remember my mother taking me to town to see Guy Gibson, the famous pilot who had bombed the dams in Germany (i.e. the leader of the Dam Busters squadron). His car pulled up outside what is now H.L. Brown, the jewellers, and he got out. He was a handsome man.

I passed the 11-Plus and went to secondary school. Imagine nowadays letting your children leave the house with their gas masks and wondering if you would ever see them again. Before the War, married women were not allowed to be teachers. The War changed that.

At age 11, I became very ill. My mother found me wandering, saying that I was lost in a forest. She called in Dr Billington. He came and said to my mother "If Greta is still alive in the morning I will send her to hospital". I went in the children's ward at the Northern General. I had nephritis and Bright's Disease – a kidney complaint. I remember my mother and Lily, our next door neighbour, coming to see me. They were not allowed in the ward and had to stand at the window, which was covered in some sticky material to stop broken glass (from bomb blast). I don't remember much in the way of Christmas presents. I found a book on the top of the wardrobe in my parents' bedroom about English heroines. I remember the story of Grace Darling. I think I had read it by the time Christmas came.

Most of my uncles were in the War. One was quite old, with only one eye, but he served in Burma. My father was on Russian convoys. One uncle was on HMS Undine, one of the first ships to be sunk, but he was rescued by the Germans and was a prisoner of war for most of the War. After his release from the War, my father brought home his demob suit and his sailor suit. He lit a bonfire in the garden and burnt them.

***Margaret Walker**, also in Sheffield, describes many of the details of daily life, such as the blackout, rationing and 'make do and mend'. Like others who experienced wartime shortages, she still cannot waste a thing.*

Margaret Walker

The Blackout

Black-out curtains – "Put that light out!"
Street lights three-quarters covered over (yet we understand that despite these precautions, from the air a city looked ablaze with light).
Torches had to be covered. We felt no fear walking down to St. Vincent's Youth Club in the dark with half a torch. You could do that in those days.

Rationing

Each person had a ration book. There was much less food, and we grew our own in the allotment - potatoes, cabbage, apples – lots of digging. We had to collect water from the stream and were more interested in the insects and frogs. Mum managed meals on 2ozs butter a week, 3 ozs sugar, 2ozs lard, 4ozs tea, 2 rashers of bacon, and a quarter pound of meat a week, plus potted meat from the tripe shop. These were the rations per person per week.

We had to queue for fruit and veg. One day there was a rumour of oranges – we eventually got one between us. No bananas (I found out I was allergic to them when they came back). Sweets were nil at first, then rationed to half a pound a week, later three quarters of a pound and in 1953 one pound – too much!

Mother saved up tea coupons and took them up to old ladies on the hill who did not need clothing coupons. She gave them tea in exchange for the clothing coupons and had to buy them! That way she could make our clothes and buy school uniform with the coupons.

Youth Organisations
We were obliged to join Guides, Scouts or other youth work – 'doing your bit'. We learnt a lot in Guides, spent time in the woods learning about flowers, trees and birds. Then progressed to Morse Code, sending messages to each other, then onto badges. I started a patrol in my school, called 'Robin'. In Guides we had to learn how to march, do 'left turns' smartly, 'Right about turn' and 'left, right' – we never had to use it. It reminds me now of Hitler Youth!

School
Our school had to move to Fulwood Road School for a whole year till the old school was repaired, and it was much nicer in Fulwood! We still had sports days in the convent grounds, which we enjoyed.

In school we had to practise 'alerts' and put on our gas masks which we carried everywhere, even to the Pictures. In films the British always won, but we also saw sad stories of airmen killed in battle.

Cooking
I learnt how to cook in Domestic Science, using dried eggs and dried milk – butterfly buns were good! I'll never forget rice pudding in school dinners made with dried skimmed milk, with a nun standing over me, making me eat it! She had to give way in the end.

Lessons and Exams
Sleeping back in the house after the year in the shelter I slept much better, in time for exams – School Certificate. Every notebook was lined to divide the margin and not waste paper. I am still very economical and can't waste paper or envelopes.

Make do and Mend
I learnt how to sew, how to make clothes by hand and cut down a dress to make one for a child, or re-style one which was too small for me. I made a sundress for tennis out of a small dress, and also learnt darning and making patterns. I found art and other creative tasks very helpful, because it took my mind off the War.

Other recollections
We played a card game in which the cards had the pictures and names of all the aircraft, British and German. This enabled us to learn and identify which was which. It was rather odd when, for instance, the Heinkel won over our Lancaster and Spitfire!

We were very patriotic and followed the news.

I was 14-years-old and all my teenage years were in the War, so we got used to the conditions.

Muriel Jackson *adds another snippet to this, concerning rations and schooling which is explained in more detail by our next contributor.*

Muriel Jackson

I don't recall ever being hungry because my mother had learned how to make a good meal out of very little, during the years Dad was out of work. We grew vegetables in the garden and Mum would go out into the countryside collecting berries, nettles etc and she made her own bread. Whilst our school was being reinforced and shelters built, our schooling was usually in small groups within various pupils' homes, as this was thought safer than our all being together in one building. It was called Home Service.

Beryl Harrison *gives some details about the practice of 'Home Service' schooling, which several other contributors also remember.*

Beryl Harrison

Three weeks after the outbreak of the Second World War on 3rd September, 1939, I celebrated my fifteenth birthday. I was due to return to school two days later at the end of the summer holiday, but my school (Abbeydale Girls' Grammar) was closed, being immediately taken over as an ARP Centre. Eventually the school organized 'Home Service', which meant that groups of about eight girls were delegated to have lessons at the houses of girls' parents who lived locally and had suitable accommodation. I think I went two mornings a week with about two hours teaching on each occasion. The rest of the time, we studied on our own at home with work that was sent out to us. After several weeks of this arrangements were made for us to go to

High Storrs School and a few weeks later our own school re-opened. Not all the girls returned as I suppose they, and their parents, thought it a waste of time when they could be doing war work. The result was that my class of thirty girls was reduced to only eight.

Pat Crellin*, living in Birmingham remembers her parents briefly housing a little Jewish girl who had escaped from Germany on the Kindertransport. She herself was almost evacuated to the USA.*

Pat Crellin

My memories of 1939 are a little vague but we were aware of the rumblings of war. The Nazi menace became more real when, as a result of my mother's attendance at the local Adult School, we were asked by the organizer, Miss Cadbury of the Quaker chocolate family, to give a home to a Jewish girl, a little older than myself. Together with her sister, Fella had escaped from Germany on the Kindertransport scheme. I think that they had been housed with most other children elsewhere in the city before being placed individually in homes. They both left the area some time later and I understand that they met up with their mother and eventually settled in Israel.

In September 1939 I was on holiday with my mother (our first ever away from home) when my school was evacuated from Birmingham. It was my 12th birthday and I did not want to be evacuated! For a few months I had no schooling until Miss Cadbury offered to tutor me at her home. In 1940 our school returned to the city and to the bombing of course. I remember the buses having a fuel gas trailer behind them because of the shortage of petrol. If we came to a hill, we had to get out and walk up to rejoin it at the top!

When the bombing continued and it also seemed likely that Britain would be invaded, the Government arranged for some children to be evacuated to Canada and the United States for safety. I was registered, health checked and was awaiting my turn for this when we were shocked to learn that one of the liners taking children on this scheme had been torpedoed in the Atlantic and sank with all on board. The scheme was then abandoned.

Londoner ***Dorothy Smith*** *spent most of the War in the Worcestershire countryside with her mother and sister, billeted with families who became lifelong friends. Her war sounds positively idyllic!*

Dorothy Smith

Early in 1940 my father was in the RAF, my mother, younger sister Evelyn and myself, were still at home in Woodford, East London, on the edge of Epping Forest. I took and passed the scholarship (later called the 11-Plus), and at Easter was evacuated with my new school to Kettering. Sometime that year my mother's friend, Mrs Echart and her two daughters were evacuated to Wichenford in Worcestershire, where they stayed for several years with Eve and Albert Hiams and their son Denis. Before long, a couple across the road from the Hiams, Mr and Mrs Whatmore, offered to take my mother, sister and myself to stay with them. We called the Hiams Uncle Albert and Auntie Eve, and Mrs Echart was Aunt Peg to us.

This was the start of a memorable and enjoyable period of my life. Our two households were like one big happy family. Not having gas, electricity or running water was quite a novelty. At the Whatmores' we had an indoor bathroom, but I cannot recall how we filled the bath. The toilet was flushed using a bucket of water, which you filled from the pump in the front garden. The Hiams' toilet was 'the little house round the corner' next to the pig-sty, with a bucket needing regular emptying.

At Easter 1941 I was transferred to Worcester Secondary School, travelling there by bus or bicycle daily, whilst the younger ones walked to the village school. Discipline on the bus was strict, with a prefect on duty ready to report any misdemeanours. Despite the War, school uniform was strictly adhered to, those black stockings even in summer with our grey cotton dresses, though later we were allowed to wear white socks.

We all had a wonderful time. We went fishing in pools, caught newts with a worm on a bent hook, climbed trees, slid on ice in winter, and went rabbiting with Uncle Albert and his ferrets. We picked raspberries, black and red currants and blackberries, and I believe the children at the village school were given a week off for this purpose.

Although food was rationed, I never remember being hungry. Auntie Eve kept chickens, and there was a pig, which I think we had to have a special licence to kill. One Christmas we were fattening up a goose for dinner on the big day. When the time came to kill it we children hid at the far end of the orchard, vowing we were not going to eat our Christmas dinner, but of course, we did!

Most evenings the adults played cards and we children loved paper and pencil games. Sometimes Auntie Eve would play the piano and we would all gather round for a sing-song, and at Christmas we went carol-singing round the houses. We attended church on Sunday mornings and I was in the Girl Guides.

Another memory is the village concert, never to be missed. Then there was the day the bus from Worcester got stuck on the hill and we all had to get off while the adults pushed it. Another memorable day was when there were no buses due to the snow and my mother walked all the way to Worcester and back for our groceries. So many happy memories! After we left, we kept in touch over the years as we all married, had children and grandchildren and often went back for visits. Now retired, it still feels like coming home when we return.

*Very different indeed are these amazing episodes recounted by **Bernard Johnson**, a young teenager living in Barrow-in-Furness.*

Bernard Johnson

I was 13-years-old when the War began, living in Barrow-in-Furness with my parents. I had five brothers and five sisters, but the oldest three were away in the forces. In the early part of the war there were daylight raids, and this first incident occurred at that time.

The warning siren sounded just before midday. "It will be another annoying false alarm," said my Mother, "but we'd better play safe. Take your sisters to the deep shelter and wait for me there. I'll bring baby and the battle-bag."

The "battle-bag" was a carpet-bag packed with cushions, snacks, sweets and compendium games. I harried my two younger sisters, 12 and 10 respectively, out of the house and towards Island Road which ran from the docks to Vickers Engineering Works. Our deep shelter lay at the far end of Island Road.

Scarcely had we entered the main road than we saw a Heinkel 111 bomber flying at chimney-pot height, following the railway lines down the centre of the road. Spurts of dust were rising from the tracks as the nose gunner fired seemingly at random. I stared, then yelled, "get back home, quick!" I could have saved my breath. My sisters were already halfway there!

The second incident occurred later on, after night raids began, and it involved a boy called Trevor, who was a bit of a rebel. Trevor would deliberately arrive at school just in time to miss morning prayers and disrupt the hymn. He would announce his impending arrival by rattling a stick along the bars of the playground fence. "Clang clang clatter clang".

On the morning following another German night air-raid, Trevor was, as usual, outside the playground, racing up and down and banging a thick metal "baton" against the bars. Curiously, this made little noise and Trevor was getting very angry. "Dunk dunk blop", was the best he could manage. Headmaster Robertson took one weary glance, howled "Noo-ooo", and stampeded from the hall and across the playground to confront a gobsmacked Trevor. Robertson tore the baton from his hand to hurl it away across the adjacent sports field.

That Incendiary-bomb exploded in a fine display of pyrotechnics!

*Thirteen year old **Pat Richardson** was evacuated from Manchester to a farm in the Lancashire countryside, with a three-mile walk each way to school. It was quite a culture shock for her, but on the whole, a happy one.*

Pat Richardson

I was born Patricia Prudames in Manchester in 1925. My name is French Huguenot and my parents told me it was very unusual. My childhood was a happy one in a secure middle class background with all the trappings.

When war broke out I was thirteen and a pupil at Whalley Range High School, and because of the threat of bombing in such a large conurbation, I became an evacuee. I was sent to the Rossendale Valley. This is predominantly a mill area producing cotton and cheap shoes. The girls there mostly left school at 14 years and worked in the mills. Bacup was at the top of the valley and Rawtenstall at the bottom. My friend, Jean Herring (Fishy), and I were somewhere in between at a small place called Stacksteads. We were almost the last to be chosen from the group of us huddled together in that church hall. However we were lucky because the couple that became our foster parents took us both.

They were kind people who had a smallholding from which they ran a dairy farm. They were in their late fifties and all their own children had fled the nest long ago. We were billeted in their old stone cottage that was built into a hillside and thus had no back door. The cottage consisted of one room only with a stone-flagged floor. It had a kitchen range and a large table in the middle. The back of the room was where the dairy was built into the hillside and it had a massive cold slab. Every day we walked the three miles into Rawtenstall Grammar School which we attended part-time because we had to share the building with the children already there. Our lessons were from 8.30am–1.30pm one fortnight and then alternately 1.30-5.30pm the other two weeks. I preferred the morning shift as when we arrived home our foster parents were still on their milk round. Jean and I would run into the dairy and scoop out a cup of thick yellow cream to drink. It was delicious and I can still drink double cream today, much to my downfall!

We stayed for about a year and a half. During that time I never went home. My mother visited me only once but she wrote weekly and sent money for my upkeep. Fortunately the air raids never materialised in Manchester and so eventually we returned home. When I think back to my time as an evacuee I realise what a massive culture shock it was to me, moving from middle class suburbia to a small farm with its diverse mix of people. I learned a lot from them and it showed me a side of life I never would have believed existed had I not experienced it at first hand. They had qualities you could not help but admire. It also made me appreciate home all the more when I returned.

The main focus of the War for me on my return home seemed to centre around the wireless, gripped by the heroism of Dunkirk, listening to Winston Churchill, and trying to make sense of what was happening to us all. My parents were both air raid wardens and I would sometimes accompany them on their rounds. Somehow they managed to secure me a tin hat of my own. One day we heard that the Germans were dropping bombs in our vicinity, the ones that had silk parachutes attached to them. We watched in horror as they silently floated down and then exploded. Miraculously they missed the Grammar School completely, but caused a crater in the playing fields and allotments nearby. There was no loss of life on that occasion. All the windows opposite the crater were intact but further away they were all broken. Next morning we rode our bikes around the area picking up pieces of parachute silk to take home – they made lovely underwear!

***Peter Barclay**, also in Manchester, recalls that 'war work' was the making of his mother. He also makes some interesting observations on the quality of education during and just after the War.*

Peter Barclay

I was eight-years-old when the Second World War began, an only child living with my parents in a suburb on the outskirts of Manchester. I can vaguely remember my mother with the wireless on, listening to Mr Chamberlain's broadcast that we were at war with Germany. At that time we didn't really know what war was, though there were still a lot of men about in the blue uniforms which showed they had been injured in the First World War. Our neighbour had a bad chest due to being gassed. My father had been in the Navy then, and still had his uniform in the wardrobe, but he never spoke about his wartime experiences until after my mother died in the 1960s. He had kept it bottled up for all those years, and then it began to pour forth.

The First World War had made a tremendous impact on society, and was thought to be 'the War to end all Wars'. Gas had been a big thing in the first War, so my mother warned me –"If you ever smell geraniums and there are no geraniums about, it's a gas attack. You must get a wet cloth and cover your mouth with it". In fact, both the Germans and British had stocks of gas but never used them due to fear of reprisals. A few months later we were issued with gas masks, but everyone hated them, and although at first it was drilled into you to carry them everywhere, eventually most folk left them in the wardrobe.

I think the adults must have known or suspected that war would come, in the late 1930s.

War work

My father worked in local government, in a deferred job, but took his turn at fire watching at nights. He worked for 5½ days a week in the office, and then some weekends he did a job on the buses, as a guard (Manchester-speak for conductor). He also joined the Home Guard for a while, had a uniform, brought his rifle home to clean, and went to a rifle range near Tintwhistle to practise. However, he got fed up with that and became an air raid warden, as did my granddad. They learnt how to tackle incendiary bombs and how to deal with air-raids. Father was fanatical about the blackout and kept inventing ways of improving it. One invention was a sheet of muslin covered with wet sticky stuff which adhered to the windows. It eventually turned slimy green with mould and we ripped it off as soon as possible, probably before the War ended properly. It was nice to be able to see the garden again.

At the start of the War they began to evacuate children from inner city Manchester. I recall a lady bringing them round and asking my mother if she could take two girls in. She was reluctant, but did it as a duty. They were about the same age as me, but were very rough, quite different from the nicely brought-up girls in our street. I quite liked this, but quickly discovered that they had fleas. Mum, having come from a working class background, soon cleaned them up, but she couldn't really cope with them and I think they left after two or three weeks.

What she really enjoyed was doing a National Savings round, selling stamps and certificates. She hated the rations and queuing, but loved the National Savings – it was the making of her. When the War ended and the Savings campaign was dropped, it left a big gap in her life. She had often been frustrated in what she wanted to do and later on became quite neurotic, but the War did her good.

Air Raids

We never had an Anderson Shelter, and as our house was modern it had no cellar. During the early raids we took bedding downstairs into the dining room. The heavy table was pulled into the corner by the chimney breast, which was the safest place, and dad put sheets of plywood round it. I thought it was a game getting under the table, but I remember the sounds so well. The siren wailing the 'Alert' paralysed me with fear.

By 1942-3 we had a Morrison shelter indoors. This was a sort of iron cage into which we crawled. Eventually we all slept downstairs in the same room. We had a double and a single bed, but I usually slept on the mattress under my bed. My friend had an Anderson shelter but I don't think they ever used it because it flooded. We lads would go in there with lanterns and use it as a meeting-place. I remember waking up one morning and asking Mum – "has my comic come?", but she said "No", that there had been a Blitz last night. All I was bothered about was my comic. When I looked around that morning I saw that our house was covered in clay and gravel. A bomb had dropped onto land a few minutes' walk away. A house was wrecked and the whole family killed. It could have been us. All we suffered was the result of bomb blast.

The Manchester and Liverpool Blitzes occurred in 1941-2. Our neighbour was a fireman and was sent to help at Liverpool. I went into Manchester with my parents after a raid and couldn't understand why they were pulling buildings down. It was because they were unsafe. There were hosepipes and wreckage all around Piccadilly.

School Days and Leisure Activities

I eventually went to Grammar School. I hated school dinners, so cycled three miles home every lunchtime, then returned to school on the bus. My friends and I often went for long cycle rides into the country at Alderley Edge, or took a bus to Lyme Park or the train to Stockport and then Edale and Chinley. We were about 14 or 15 years old. Our parents trusted us to look after ourselves.

Considering there was a War on, our teachers did a pretty good job. We had a very keen music teacher, Mr Brown, who made arrangements for us to have seats at Manchester Opera House in the afternoons. I really grew to love the theatre in those wartime years. On V.J. day, 1945, I saw Joyce Redman and Ralph Richardson at the Opera House in a performance of Peer Gynt.

At school we had a choir to which I belonged and also performed some Gilbert & Sullivan shows. I always had to play female parts, as we were a strictly boys-only school. You hung onto anything during the War that would provide welcome relief. It was fun to stay behind after school to rehearse, and then go home in the blackout. We had no fear of it – it was a way of life.

In some respects we didn't get a very good education. Our textbooks were old and out of date and although some teachers were young men not called up for medical reasons, others were older men called out of retirement and drafted into teaching. They didn't really want to do it. My art teacher was only in his thirties and wanted to be a fighter pilot, but was turned down for medical reasons.

Once the War ended and demobbed ex-servicemen returned to the school, the difference in the teaching stood out a mile. They were fit, young and enthusiastic, idealistic and confident, accustomed to big responsibilities, and knew what life and death were all about because of their wartime experiences. They were an incredible generation. We'd try to sidetrack them to tell us what they did in the War. One of these teachers looked different from the rest, because he had been a prisoner of war of the Japanese, and had worked on the infamous Burma Railway. He was thin and undernourished, yet wanted to get back to a normal life. He was held in the greatest respect by both masters and boys.

Afterthoughts

In 1943/4 we saw more American service people about the streets. Our relatives in New York sent us food parcels. The American influence remains in Britain to this day.

I was 14 when the War ended and 16 when I left school. I came to realise that we had been subjected to a lot of government propaganda during the War. This, coupled with Giles' cartoons, which always showed the Germans as humourless, robotic characters, goose-stepping and shouting "Heil Hitler" all the time, meant we didn't know what they were really like.

Towards the end of the War German Prisoners of War were sent out to work on the roads and the Italians on farms. They seemed pleasant enough. On the other hand, we didn't know about the concentration camps till the end of the war.

At a later stage my friend brought two Germans to have tea with us. Herr Walter had been in the Army during the War, and was quite friendly. His son, aged 15, had been brought up in the Hitler Youth and hated the British. When I appeared in my RAF uniform it did not go down well. Later Herr Walter invited me to stay with them in Germany and I got on well with his family. His daughter Brigitte had also been brought up in the Hitler Youth. She told me they were taught "The only good Englishman is a dead one". I said we'd been taught the same about the Germans. Although we got on well, there were awkward moments. For instance, she didn't want to know about the concentration camps and insisted there were still plenty of Jews around.

Not all Germans were fooled by Hitler's propaganda. My other friends in Düsseldorf did not feel the same. When Inge was five years old her father went missing on the Russian front, and never returned. At first her mother said "you must never speak to the enemy soldiers" (ie British and American soldiers in the army of occupation) but the soldiers gave chocolates to the children and eventually their mother grew to like them.

Margaret Platts *was on holiday in France when war was declared and made a hasty exit. A clever girl, she trained to become a doctor, and is one of several contributors praising teachers who took on responsibilities 'in loco parentis' beyond the call of duty, and ensured that her education was not neglected.*

Margaret Platts

I was born in 1924 in Sheffield, so I would have been 14 or 15 years of age when the War began. We lived on Harcourt Road, Crookesmoor, and I attended Western Road Primary School at Crookes and then won a scholarship to the Girls' High School.

When World War II began, I was actually on holiday in France. I was learning French at school, so I pestered my mother to ask my aunt and uncle to take me to France with them and so when War was declared in September 1939, we were on holiday in Sangatte,

Northern France. My uncle, who was a bank manager, returned to England immediately, and the rest of us followed about two weeks later. We returned on a boat full of nuns, who were all being sick over the side. I recall feeling very tough because I wasn't sick.

I travelled from London to Sheffield on my own on the train, something I had been doing since I was quite young. I vaguely knew that the High School would move to the country if war came. By the time I got back, they were already established at Cliff College, Calver. Some of the girls lived at the College, but there was not space for all of us, so my younger sister and I were lodged in the nearby village under the Government evacuee scheme. My parents paid a small sum for our board and lodging, possibly about 7s 6d a week.

We walked to and from school each day, taking sandwiches for our lunch. At weekends our parents came out on the bus to visit us and we would go for a country walk together. The house where we stayed had a bathroom and an outside toilet, as was usual, but that was okay because it was a proper flush toilet and just outside the back door. The couple we stayed with were childless, and did not seem very fond of children. They were never unkind, but we did not feel welcome. They tolerated us, but we never felt at ease there, though the food situation was better than at home, since our host had a gun and could shoot rabbits to supplement our rations. I don't think they really wanted us, and we didn't want to be there.

Apart from country walks, there was little other entertainment, but I spent much of my time studying for the School Certificate. Our lodging house backed onto the village cricket ground, and as I was keen on cricket, they let me be the scorer sometimes. The Yorkshire Cricket Team were my pin-ups at that time.

I really take my hat off to our teachers, as they also lived in at the college, and had the pastoral care of us all, including those lodging in the village. After my School Certificate exam, I wanted to stay on to sixth form and eventually become a doctor, but of course Cliff College (which had been a Methodist Bible College), had no laboratories, and I needed to study science. Therefore arrangements were made for me to join the sixth form at High Storrs Grammar School, which did have labs.

This meant that I could live at home again, and my sister was sent to new lodgings in Baslow with several other girls, where she was much happier. The Sheffield Blitz took place while I was at Calver, so although the city did have some air raids after that, we would just go downstairs. We had given up going to the cellar, which was cold and uncomfortable.

I began my medical training at Sheffield University, which meant I could still live at home, so did not have the usual student experience of living independently in another town. My mother managed to feed us all plus a student lodger, on the rations. She never 'bought under the counter' i.e. got extra food on the black market. We had plenty to eat, but the diet could be boring. I seem to remember having plums and custard five times a week for lunch at the hospital.

Sheffield Medical School was much smaller then than it is now. The number of students in each year was in the teens, so we had a more personal relationship with the lecturers. I'd say we were about half and half men and women, which was not perhaps the case before the War, but many men were away in the forces. My home was conveniently situated for the university and for many of the hospitals, e.g. Jessop's, the Children's, the Royal on West Street and the Royal Infirmary. I only had to 'live in' for certain parts of the course, such as Midwifery (Jessop's was near enough for me to pop home and get my washing done) and of course for my House Officer year.

I was working at the Royal Infirmary Casualty Department when the War ended and I don't recall joining any wild celebrations – we still had a job to do. I think the thing I missed most during the War was the chance to travel abroad. I was at an age when I really longed to travel, but neither during the War nor for some years afterwards was it possible to go abroad.

Kay Nicholson *was a colonial child, and at a very young age was called upon to undertake a heavy responsibility for younger siblings, experiencing a separation from her parents which was long both in years and distance. Again we can only marvel at the burden of care shouldered by the teachers at her boarding school.*

Kay Nicholson

My father was one of the vast number of people who administered the British Empire. He was a District Commissioner in Sudan, where he had been since 1926. When the War began, my mother, myself, younger brother Ronnie and baby sister, happened to be in England, and we were unable to return to the Sudan. Likewise my father was unable to get back to England and so we were separated. We were living in Dorset when, in 1942, my mother was informed that if she wanted to join my father, this was her last chance. She could go out on a troopship, taking the long way round the Cape, because the Mediterranean was too dangerous, and of course, she could not take the children.

I remember being in bed with my mother, who was reading 'The Secret Garden' to me, when she suddenly stopped and explained to me that she could go to join my daddy, but it was dangerous because the ship might be sunk by U-boats. Therefore we children would have to stay behind. We could go to Miss Wild's school, and she would look after us, along with her other 'colonial' pupils who had been stranded in England apart from their parents since the war began. She asked me if I could manage to look after the others, and I, being proud of being the eldest, said that I could manage. I was five years old, Ronnie was only three and our sister was a toddler.

I could understand this, but my brother at three years old, could not, and he was going through a very 'clingy' phase with our mother. He never got over the experience and never really forgave her. She later told me that if I had cried and begged her not to go, she would have stayed, but she felt quite reassured by my positive attitude. It has to be said that Ronnie cried constantly for our mother, his only comfort being sucking his thumb and holding the arm of his teddy. I'm afraid this bothered my friend Patricia and I so much that we invented a monster called Shakay (from our two names). We would hide the teddy in the airing cupboard and tell Ronnie that Shakay had taken the bear because he was crying, and would only give it back when he stopped.

Miss Wild's school was at Wimborne in Dorset and we lived there throughout the war. We could hear the bombers flying over Poole Harbour, but we thought it was fun to get out of bed and go in our pyjamas into the big air raid shelter which was equipped with bunk beds, and sleep there. The bunks were so roughly made, that the bark was still on some of the wood. It is to the credit of our teachers that we felt no fear – they made it seem like a game.

Soon after the War ended in 1945, our parents came back, bringing a new little sister. All the children at school had parents returning, and we made a big Welcome banner in front of the school and turned out with flags to welcome them. Almost immediately we were sent off to prep schools and boarding schools and our parents returned to Sudan, where they lived until the country gained independence when I was 20. We went to them for holidays and they came home on leave – that was the normal life for families involved in administering our far-flung empire.

After my mother's death, I found that she had kept a pencil-written letter from me to her, which said –

> "My dear Mummy and Daddy, I hope the ship won't singk(sic). I hope you will like being with Daddy and Daddy like being with you" – and at the end, the proud boast that – "Ronnie is awefully(sic) good boy, with love from your lovely Kay".
>
> It is dated 23rd March 1942.

Cliff Crellin's *family in Liverpool endured a good deal of bombing but as they also had relatives on the Isle of Man, they found that travelling between the two locations by ferry could be almost equally perilous.*

Cliff Crellin

Outbreak of war and evacuation

In 1939 I was at a boys' Secondary School in Liverpool. When it became obvious that War with Germany was imminent all sorts of Air Raid Precautions (ARP) were made for our big cities. As a major seaport Liverpool with transatlantic links was clearly going to be a target. Air raid shelters were constructed, blackout curtains hung up, barrage balloons were put in place near key targets to deter dive bombers, but the action that affected me most at that time as a 12 year old schoolboy, was that we were to be evacuated to a safer area, I did not know where! My nine year old younger brother was still at Elementary School and was sent to the village of Brymbo near Wrexham on September 1st (two days before war was declared). I went with the rest of my school by train to Bangor, a largely Welsh speaking town in North Wales on 3rd September (I still have the card but not the gas mask). In addition to one small suitcase we were told to take a metal enamelled mug. The result was that these mugs soon became in short supply and were difficult to buy anywhere in the city. Later our hosts said they were disgusted that it was thought they drank out of that sort of cup in Wales.

So the day war broke out we arrived in Bangor at 11am and waited in a school gymnasium until about 4pm when we were taken in pairs by a billeting officer who knocked on doors asking the householders to take us in. The two grammar schools had been allocated to Upper Bangor while the two elementary schools were in Lower Bangor. Eventually, after some understandable hesitation we were accepted by a family of Quakers: a University Lecturer and his wife and their own two children. It was a large house and they had a resident maid; this was quite a culture shock for me with my working class background.

We went to school for long afternoons, the Welsh boys going in the morning. We stayed in Bangor until Christmas when we came home for a few days. But, because Bangor had become overcrowded with evacuees we were sent back to Llanfairfechan, a small village along the North Wales coast . At first over 20 of us were housed in a small boarding house but after a couple of weeks two of us were billeted in a four-roomed cottage on the hillside at the top of the village with an unemployed man and his wife. We later discovered that he was the local poacher! We would sometimes have wild duck or pheasant for a meal but more often much simpler food when he was less successful! They were very kind to us and gave us two of their rooms as a bedroom and as a living room. This was probably easier because their young son could not speak English and the father was not very fluent himself.

During that year very little happened on the home front and many evacuated children and their families wanted to be together again as most had been homesick at some time during their stay. Gradually most of the schoolchildren returned home and by the end of May 1940 our school in Liverpool was almost back to normal again, but most of the younger teachers had been called up for military service.

News from the front

During this time I heard from my uncle who had joined the Army under age in the First World War. He had been imprisoned and sent to work in salt mines, which adversely affected his eyes. On his return he joined the

Territorial Army as a Royal Army Service Corps (RASC) driver and in 1939 was sent to France with the British Expeditionary Force (BEF) but because of a road accident in the blackout, he was taken to hospital. It was from there that he wrote to me hinting at where he was because the censor would have 'blue pencilled' any place name. After Dunkirk collapsed he escaped through St.Nazaire but as his turn to embark came he saw the fully loaded Cunard liner, Lancastria, sunk by dive-bombers. This sudden advance by the German Army did not take place until the summer of 1940. However after the fall of France the bombers now had airfields in the occupied countries nearer to Britain and the bombing began.

Bombing

On the clear evening of September 3rd 1940 I had been with my friends playing out in the street until bedtime. That night their house was among those destroyed by a bomb and all six members of the family were killed. The following morning I saw their bodies being taken away in sacks. The front of our house was destroyed also. There had been no air raid warning siren and I was in bed but, living in terraced houses with backyards and no gardens, we did not have Anderson shelters. Later in the War Morrison table shelters were offered to such families, but we preferred to sit under the stairs. My father was on night duty on the docks so my mother and I were alone at the back of the house when an auxiliary policeman came in and walked up the stairs. She had to get very angry before he would come down. I was surprised at this attitude from someone who was usually a law-abiding woman but she explained that there had been rumours about looting of bombed premises by members of these auxiliary organisations.

The night following the bombing we stayed at a friend's house and that too was damaged and the house next door set alight by incendiary bombs. I helped pull down curtains to limit the spread of the fires, and was surprised but pleased to be congratulated on my energetic vandalism!

School continued – even when the windows were blown out! From time to time in the early part of the War when the air raid siren went we would have to run down to the brick shelters built in the school yard. At home if the 'All Clear' siren went after midnight we were allowed to go in to school an hour later.

Mined at sea

When Christmas came I was sent for 'a rest' to my grandparents who lived in the Isle of Man. Food rationing was less stringent there. However, soon after the steamer had left the landing stage and sailed up the Mersey Channel, it set off three acoustic mines which had been dropped during the air raid the night before. Luckily for us, the only damage the ship received on that voyage was to loosen plates on the hull; but it was the most frightening experience of my life, even more than the bombing. For the rest of the War the ferry service between Douglas and Liverpool was withdrawn and the fishing port of Fleetwood was used instead.

Starting work and Military training

I left school in 1943 at 16 and began work in a Barclays Bank near the Pier Head. Occasionally the King or Churchill would pay a surprise visit to the office building over the road which we later learned was the HQ of Western Approaches from which the Battle of the Atlantic was operated. The only other event to break the monotony was the day a large contingent of U.S. troops arrived. Our bank held the account for the U.S. Army but wartime secrecy meant that we had no warning that they would be arriving and so we did not have enough cash to pay them. I was sent with a couple of bank messengers across to the nearby branch of the Bank of England with several empty suitcases to collect £150,000 (about £3million? in today's money). On the way back we passed the coffee shop so went in to have the morning break we had missed! When we came out American jeeps were flying up and down the road looking for us! But all that the head cashier said to me when we returned to the bank past the armed U.S. guard was "Do have your break before you go next time!"

About that time also I joined the Air Training Corps which met in a school after work. It was compulsory for 16-year-olds to register and they were urged to undergo cadet training of some sort. Very occasionally a dance would be arranged. Towards the end of one such evening a fellow cadet, who was very shy and bashful, asked me if I would join him and a girl whom he knew and who had somehow persuaded him to walk her home. I made it clear that obviously the girl liked him and that I had no wish to spoil a budding romance! But as he obviously needed some moral support I eventually agreed to his pleas to accompany them part of way along the road. We met outside the hall and because of the blackout I did not see the young lady who joined us. All three of us set off chatting away cheerfully until I realised that George was no longer joining in the conversation! So now there were only two of us in the blackout never having seen each other before ! In the circumstances we agreed that I should accompany her to her home. She explained that her mother would be waiting up for her and so she did not usually invite a boyfriend in. However she was intrigued to see who it was who had walked her home! Mother jumped to the wrong conclusion and when Doreen was sent into the kitchen to make the cocoa, mother interrogated me on my life and prospects and finally made it quite clear that they were not good enough for her daughter! Thus not for the only time I was weighed in the balance and found wanting!

The serious business
In 1944 when I was 17, I volunteered and was accepted for the Fleet Air Arm (Navigator) but the War ended before I began my training proper and I was remustered to another branch of the Navy, ending up ironically in 801 Naval Air Squadron, moving frequently between naval Air Stations and the aircraft carrier HMS Implacable.

***Cliff Crellin** has saved three of his 'Letts Schoolboy Diaries' from the war years. The following are transcripts of some entries from the years 1940 and 1941. The brief entries jumble together the ordinary with the* *extraordinary in a most amazing way and are all the more remarkable for that.*

Cliff Crellin – 1940 Letts Schoolboy Diary (extracts)
Cliff was 13 years old, living in Liverpool

27th May – Aunty to Lewis's for a job. No vacancies. School. Dunkirk.

29th May – Scouts. School. 'Mona's Queen' sunk at Dunkirk. (**explanation** – Mona's Queen was an Isle of Man ferry and Cliff's granddad had been its captain until 2 years previously)

17th June –France asks Germany for an armistice. School.

18th June – Prizegiving. Lord Mayor came to school.

4th September – 2.20 a.m. Bomb destroyed 4 houses opposite us. Four girls Birches and Mother killed. Mr Birch injured. Our house wrecked.

6th September – Found out that Miss Singleton next door killed. Died in Hospital.

1st November – school. Air raid postponed my dinner for 1 hour.

2nd November – Played football against 4A, won 7-5. Air raid interrupted.

7th Nov – school. King and Queen in Liverpool.

8th Nov – air raid as usual.

15th Nov – school. Ruthless Nazi attack by dive bombers on Coventry. 200 killed.

21st Nov – Heavy raid on Liverpool on scale of Coventry city. More killed.

22nd Nov – Raid

23rd Nov – played Rugby practice

21st December – found a piece of shrapnel in our yard from raid last night. Dear old St. Nicholas Church gone.

23rd Dec – come to Isle of Man on 'Victoria'. 3 mines blew up near us 20 minutes from Bar. It shook the ship. Waited from 1.15 p.m. to 5.15 p.m. for boat. Arrived 9.30 p.m.

27th Dec – Auntie Edna went on the 'Victoria' back to Liverpool. But when it came it hit a mine. Smashed rudders. Was pulled into Liverpool.

Cliff Crellin – 1941 Letts Schoolboy Diary (extracts)
Cliff (aged 14) was living in Liverpool

14th January – snowed a bit. Started school again worse luck! No air raids.

15th Jan – school. Raid at 9.30 p.m.-10.15p.m. Air raid in early morning or tomorrow 2.50-3.20 a.m.

16th Jan – school. I can walk on ice in park lake. Mother went to Lewis's cafe.

19th Jan – snowed heavily. I had Dad's ARP gum boots on. I can walk anywhere now in drifts.

22nd Jan – slushy. School. British forces captured Tobruk tonight. Liverpool men there.

1st Feb – went to Pictures. Saw an awful Picture. Air raid siren 2.15-3.35p.m. First raid since 15th Jan.

17th March – school. Mr 'Fanny' Whitehouse was killed last Wednesday.

18th March – Mr Whitehouse was buried today and masters went to funeral.

1st May – 11.55 p.m. to 4 a.m. Heavy blitz. School.

2nd May – worst blitz of war on us 12 to 4 again. Lost a window.

3rd May – one of the worst air raids ever launched on Britain was given us by Hitler the rat. Lost more windows.

4th May – Another bad blitz, not as bad as Saturday night though 12-4. Lewis's store burnt out.

5th May – was late for school as went to bed after raid at 4.30 a.m. but it did not matter as school has lost most of windows from back part on Saturday night. Helped in clearing debris in school and acted as messenger.

7th May – went to school yesterday and today at 10 a.m.

20th October – school. Auntie Clara came at 5.30p.m from Isle of Man. Air raid to greet her 8.55 to 11.45 p.m. Rather heavy.

25th October – played football. Air raid 9 to 12.

19th December – went for my supplementary clothing coupons card. Got Mother and Dad's Christmas present.

25th December – Had a good meal. Turkey.

31st Dec – went to Mr Partington's party after working in Bakehouse. Had a small glass of Elderberry Wine. **(by this time Cliff was working part-time in his Uncle's Bakehouse to earn pocket money)**

In Uniform

In spite of all the dangers and the high risk of being killed or wounded, many thousands of people, both men and women, volunteered to enlist in the Forces, even some of those who were in reserved occupations and would not have been called up.

The stories in this section are from people who spent all or part of the War in one of the various services. Many of them were very young but they were all keen to join up as soon as they could. They mention danger, discomfort, cold and hunger, all of which they appear to have accepted without question and to have borne stoically.

But some people found their years in the Forces to be genuinely happy and enjoyable. Some saw parts of the country they had never travelled to before while others encountered Americans and black people for the first time. A couple of them met their future husbands.

*Although **Bill Alty** was in a reserved occupation he had a desire to go to sea and so he bent the truth about his occupation so that he could join the Royal Naval Volunteer Reserve (RNVR). Despite his experiences in the Navy and taking part in the D-Day landings, he feels that civilians had a harder time during the War than those in the Services.*

Bill Alty – Royal Navy

I was 16 in 1939, living in Ravensthorpe, Dewsbury. I was training as an apprentice draughtsman with a company making equipment for the RAF. At 17½ years old I went to join up but the Huddersfield recruiting office wouldn't take me as I was in a reserved occupation. I had a desire to go to sea which may be due to my grandfather having been a seafaring man, though he moved to Dewsbury from Liverpool in order to get his family away from the sea. I also thought that it would be nice to be somewhere where I knew where my bed was, and had someone else to cook my meals.

I tried the Merchant Navy but they wanted men with experience so I went to the Royal Navy recruiting office in Leeds and told them I was a costing clerk. They never checked up on this so I was in. I really wanted to be an engineer but the only jobs open at the time were either a steward or signalman. As I had been in the Scouts and learned both the Morse code and Semaphore, I opted for signalman.

First they sent me to HMS Collingwood, a training base at Fareham near Gosport which lasted about 12 weeks. Then they asked me to choose whether I wanted to go on big ships (i.e. from a destroyer up) or small ships (e.g. patrol boats and minesweepers). I picked minesweepers. Next I went to Lowestoft, a patrol service centre, which was a sort of holding place where we awaited our draft. It was here I had my first lucky escape. Every Monday night I used to go to a dance at the NAAFI canteen which was situated above Burton's the Tailor's shop. The week after I got my draft chit to move on, a bomb hit it on the Monday night and many Wrens and sailors were killed. I would certainly have been there had I not got my draft to Granton, near Edinburgh, which was a minesweeper base.

My first ship was HMS Hildina, a converted trawler. The signalman was ill so I went as stand-in. One night I was asleep in my hammock when I heard over the tannoy something about lifeboats. Almost before I knew it, I was out of the hammock, up on deck and jumping into a lifeboat, only to find that the message had been to the effect that a lifeboat had come loose from the davit. I wasn't allowed to forget that boob for weeks.

It was not long before I was moved to another ship – HMS Resound. With a name like that I thought it must be at least a battleship but in fact it was the smallest trawler I had ever seen. Our job was to clear a channel of mines for the Russian convoys. It was a dangerous task and cold up there but in many ways my luck was in. The skipper was a former trawler skipper whose rank was Skipper RNR, a specially created commission. He could not read or write very well. Being the signalman I was his reader and writer, interpreting all the messages that came, ordering stores etc. He was very grateful.

After 12 to 18 months a signal arrived asking for recommendations for a commission. The Skipper asked me if I'd like to be put forward and I agreed. Then he asked if I would write out a recommendation and read it to him and he'd sign it. I must be the only man who wrote his own recommendation. A week or two later both of us were called for interview by a Royal Navy Captain. My Skipper was asked as many questions as me. I was accepted and then went to Lowestoft for an interview with the Commodores' Board. They asked daft questions like: "What does your father do?" and "How would you cope with a £25 Mess bill?" As £25 was a fortune then, I said I'd collapse with shock. "But wouldn't your father pay it for you?" was their response. I told them my father had not got that kind of money.

Next came a 12-week course in seamanship, pilotage and power of command. There were 24 of us in the class and only four would go forward for a commission. I was one of the four. One of the tutors, a Lieutenant, called me and said: "You've got to change your accent". I replied, "Look, I am 20. I was born with my accent and am proud of it. You'll either take me with it or lose me". I never heard any more about my accent.

So, I got through and joined with others for a 12-week Commission Course at Lochailort near Mallaig. Ten subjects were covered, but every day began the same. We'd be up at 6 a.m. running a 2 mile track, which included a river, twice over, and this was from January to March. Then the assault course which ended in mud. We were freezing cold, wet, and often lost a boot in the mud. Then we climbed up An Stac (a big hill) and then we had breakfast. Washed and changed, we commenced our studies until 3 p.m. with a 1-hour lunch break. At 3p.m.

we did all the exercise again. I weighed 11½ stone at the start of the course and 9 stones by the end of it.

During that time, as I later found out, my mother was rushed to hospital with a burst appendix which was a serious matter then – she could have died. My dad was in a dilemma. He didn't want to bother me while I was on this important course but if my mother was dying he knew I'd have wanted to see her. In the end he kept it to himself and she recovered. I took all the exams and passed.

After I got my commission I went back to Granton to see my old ship. When I asked them: "Is Resound in?" the reply came "Sorry lad, she hit a mine and it is not known if anyone was saved". I never heard any more about the fate of my former colleagues.

Now I was a Sub-Lieutenant, RNVR and was sent to Portsmouth to learn such useful things as which way to pass the port at dinner. One day I was Officer of the Day in Portsmouth Barracks, a major headquarters, which meant I could easily be sitting next to an Admiral. The job involved organising the Division and running the show for that day. Luckily I had a Petty Officer who had done the job for years and ensured I made no great errors. One of my tasks was to visit the cells to ask the prisoners if they had any complaints. The Petty Officer told me to put my head in and draw it out quickly or it would be trapped in the door - there was no time for anyone to complain. Naval regulations decreed that the officer must be in the cell when the question was asked.

I was next sent to a shore vessel, HMS President, which was an office unit set up to organise the Combined Operations and training of small landing craft for D-Day. From President we were drafted to Salcombe in Devon where we formed flotillas of craft practising for D-Day. We practised landing and repelling boarders. One time we did a 20-mile march from Salcombe to Bigbury Bay and by the time we arrived we were not in a fit state to repel anyone, so we made sure we captured the local pub for a start.

D-Day

At Southampton we loaded up with Bailey bridging and 3.7 anti-aircraft ammunition and went to Bosham Creek, near Chichester, to await orders. We were there for about three to four weeks. Our initial instructions to set sail on 4th June were cancelled due to bad weather. We then received instructions ordering us to sail at 6 p.m. on 5th June. After leaving Bosham we began circling the Nab Tower just off Chichester, hundreds of us circling around it. Then we set off across the Channel. You followed the guy in front, guided only by a tiny purple light on the stern of the ship in front, until we separated to various parts of the beaches.

We were loaded pretty deep, only nine inches out of the water and there was a stiff breeze. We had each been assigned our own bit of beach in Normandy on which to land but when I got to my allocated spot another craft had got there first and had hit a mine which had blown its bows off. So, I had to find a different bit of beach. I was glad I hadn't got to my patch first, because we should have hit the mine and as we were much smaller the damage would have been more serious.

The conditions on the beach on arrival were somewhat chaotic. Our own ships were shooting at the enemy defences ashore over our heads and a large gun at Cabourg up the coast towards Le Havre was shelling the beach. That particular gun caused problems many days later on when things had quietened down for crews of ships which were beached awaiting high tide used to play cricket on the beach and complained about the Cabourg gun ruining the pitch.

We got rid of our load and set off back to England, loaded up again and set off to return to Normandy but a storm came up and we caught it halfway across. It swamped the ship and the engines stopped working. Because the order was not to stop for anyone in trouble, we just drifted for two days in a westerly direction but had no idea how far we travelled. Then I saw an RAF plane overhead, so I grabbed the lamp and signalled to him for help. Not long after, we saw a German E-boat alongside a small oil tanker which it had captured. As it was obvious that we would be next to be boarded we prepared to defend ourselves by each having to hand several of the hand grenades we were in fact loaded with. To our amazement, the E-boat suddenly took off to the west. When I looked east I realized why, as I saw that a British frigate was approaching in the distance. This had scared the German boat away. Unfortunately the frigate was not able to tow us home but did tow us to the tanker. That was when we found that the tanker's wheelhouse had been damaged and the steering gear and compass wrecked.

The tanker's engines were working, so we repaired the steering gear and I transferred to the tanker which we used to tow our own boat home. We only had one compass between the two boats so had to pass the bearings to and fro as it is not possible to transfer a compass from one vessel to another. It took two days to reach port. During that time we lived on tinned tomatoes. We got a write-up in the local paper and I was mentioned in despatches. Following calculations carried out using our ship's log of courses steered, and period of time on those courses, along with the information gained from the frigate, it was determined that we must have sailed over some 10 to 14 miles of minefields in a boat loaded with thousands of gallons of fuel and towing another loaded with hand grenades. After that we returned to Normandy and spent the next few weeks ferrying equipment from coasters lying off the beach, our only problem being the Cabourg gun.

Then we handed over the boats to the Army and came home to prepare for the invasion of Japan. I joined a big landing ship used for tanks as Navigating Officer and was promoted to Lieutenant RNVR. We trained on some flat beaches in Scotland and then set off to Cochin in India where the Japanese invasion force was assembling. When we got to Suez our diesel generators kept breaking down. Two of the three had to be working in order for us to go to sea but from Port Said onwards we never had more than one generator working. I am sure that the engineer made this happen in order to delay us. We never left there as the atom bombs were dropped and Japan surrendered.

As the tank landing craft was being returned to the USA I was then drafted to a minesweeper called HMS Sarka, as Skipper, and worked in the Adriatic for a while before receiving orders to return the vessel to Plymouth when it was to be handed back to the South African owners.

I tried to stay in the Navy. They offered me a Class B release which I refused, then a Class A release. I asked if I could stay and was told, "Yes, for one year, and then we review the situation to see if we still need you". I decided this might be a wasted year, as if I had to return to civilian life, I needed to get back to school as soon as possible to pick up where I left off. So back I went and found myself at the age of 24, sitting next to 16-year-olds at night school.

On the whole, I think those of us in the Services had an easier time than the civilians. We were fed much better, and although we were in danger some of the time, we did not have to face the daily bombing which was the lot of so many civilians.

The strain of the air raids during the War means that even today ***Faith Woodmansey*** *still feels a shiver when she hears a siren on the television or radio. In 1942 she joined the Women's Royal Naval Service (WRENs) aged* *just 17½ and was thrilled to learn that her uniform included black silk stockings.*

Faith Woodmansey - WRENS (Fleet Air Arm)

In 1939 I was living in Southsea, Hampshire. In September I was due to start at a new school based in Southsea, but because it was apparent that war was imminent, the school was moved to an area near Petersfield. I joined it there just as war was declared. We did have School Certificate exams, taken in the winter term so our revising did not spoil the summer term for us!

At 17-years-old I left school and at 17½ I joined the WRENS - that was in June 1942. We started at Mill Hill for just two weeks and I was told I was to be a radio mechanic, despite the fact that my only relevant exam result was a good mark in maths. From there we went to a big house called Hornby House (the home of the maker of Hornby trains) in Cheyne Walk, Chelsea Embankment, where we lived for nine months while studying at Battersea Polytechnic. It was a lovely house overlooking the Thames.

We were issued with our uniforms: navy skirt, jacket, white shirts with stiff collars, black tie, flat cap, black shoes and best of all, black silk stockings. We also had two navy blue shirts for working gear and bell-bottom trousers. These were intended for men so we had great fun cutting some bits out and sewing up the waists to fit the female figure. My first pay packet was 12 shillings and I felt: 'I'm free at last, I'm a wage-earner'.

The training course was very intensive: three years compressed into nine months. There were no breaks or holidays and we had a professor from Cambridge University trying to teach us physics, maths and electronics. It was very hard work, and more so for me, because I had not done physics at school, nor the Higher Certificate like the other girls. There was the added strain of air raids and even today I still shiver when I hear a siren on television or radio. Every night for weeks we heard the bombs raining down and saw the searchlights criss-crossing the river. Soon after we left, the house was damaged by a bomb and partly destroyed. We also learned drill and marching. On the way back to the Poly we would kick our hats in the park.

When the course ended, we were given one week's leave and then sent to HMS Ariel at Culcheth, near Warrington, for three months of practical hands-on training. After the luxury of Hornby House, it looked awful. We were accommodated in long Nissen huts, 36 to a hut with just one cast-iron stove in the middle for heating. The ground was muddy and cold and we were up at 6 a.m. every morning for P.T. (physical training) and in the evening there was 'square-bashing'. In a way it was easier for me because it was like an extension of boarding school but for girls who had never left home before it was a nasty shock. I was amazed to see 20-year-olds in tears because they missed their homes and families.

At Culcheth, unlike Hornby House, there were men and women mixed. I was the youngest there and very green. People were very good to me – I was treated perfectly by the men. The other girls were older, and clever, having their Higher School Certificates, but they came from all over the country, and at first I had a job coping with the many different accents. Here we were taken to a foundry and taught how to make our own tools, some of which I still have. There were lectures on the various radio sets with valves, coils, circuits and resistors and we learned how to splice a rope, solder wiring and how to use an ammeter. We were given circuits to repair and taught the difference between radio wavelengths.

At the end of the three months, there was an exam, and this time it was the Final. Then we had a week's home leave to await our final posting. Now that we were qualified, we became Petty Officers, with a raise in salary. My official posting was to HMS Merlin, at Donibristle, near Inverkeithing, Fife. Travelling by train with my heavy tool kit and suitcase was a nightmare. The trains were so full you usually had to stand, or sit on the tool box. Our accommodation was in a mansion called Fordell House, previously owned by the Duke of Buckingham. We slept in large dormitories with about 30 girls in bunk beds but the ceilings had beautiful plaster decorations.

We were trained in the use of the Morse code by an old hand called Stripey who always had tea brewing in the hut, and who pulled no punches. You could always tell his messages by the way he banged down the keys. Our base was on the Firth of Forth so that we could service the radios of aircraft from aircraft carriers which would fly into our airfield to be checked and repaired. The fitters would check the engines and repair bullet holes and the engineers would replace the bombs or torpedoes. We would take out the radio sets, which were so heavy it took two of us to lift them, bench test them in the hut, repair them if necessary and then replace them in the aircraft.

Once we had fitted the radios into the planes, we tested those with more than one cockpit in the air, including the canvas-clad bi-plane, the Swordfish. There was an extra line fixed to the harness to make sure you did not fall out! Other planes included Hurricanes, Spitfires and Fulmers and later some American planes whose radios were more modern and much smaller. On one occasion we worked non-stop for 24 hours on Fulmers which helped in the sinking of a German battleship. We became adept at using tools and working in awkward positions. Being quite small I was chosen to climb into the small hatch in the body of the Spitfires, lying on all the control lines to fix junction boxes.

Edinburgh was the nearest city and we would go there for bookshops, cinemas and theatres, running down the steps at Waverley station to catch the last train back. It was there that I first learnt to enjoy opera. At the camp we would have dances and it felt awful at first, all the women sitting along the wall at one side, pretending that we were not waiting to be asked to dance. Having come straight from boarding school, I had no civilian clothes and had to borrow a dress from my cousin. I did have one or two boyfriends, and at first I insisted I would never go out with an officer - having decided that the class system should be abolished, it was against my principles. I eventually married an ex-army officer instead! I was still terribly naive and when the Americans at a nearby camp asked the WRENS to visit, I went out of curiosity because I had never seen an American before. I didn't realise they were just looking for girlfriends. A kindly, middle-aged man took me under his wing (I think he had daughters my age) and when he asked why I'd come I said it was because I wanted to see what Americans were like.

I was in the Fleet Air Arm long enough to get my Three Years' Stripe, and was demobbed from Yeovilton in 1946.

Evelyn Hughes *also joined the WRENS but she was sent to work at Bletchley Park. There she helped to set up the Bombes, the machines designed to break the German codes.*

Evelyn Hughes – WRENS

At the age of 18 in December 1943 I signed up for the WRENS. It was the only part of His Majesty's Armed Forces that was not subject to military discipline. It was a very élite service and the initial interview was more to do with our background, education, connections with the Services etc, rather than our intelligence. Preliminary training was at the Methodist College, in Roundhay, Leeds. Here we learned naval rules and regulations, got measured for our uniforms and found out the great news that this was the only service where we were allowed to wear silk stockings.

At this point we underwent intelligence tests for our suitability for Bletchley Park itself. I passed and was sent to Eastcote Air Field, where I received my final training that lasted about six weeks. I was finally dispersed to living quarters in a beautiful old house in Steeple Claydon, Buckinghamshire which supposedly had been a former 'love nest' of Edward V111. I actually worked at Adstock (Bucks), which were former stables, very remote and full of mice.

The machines (we called them Bombes) were set to work 24 hours per day, seven days a week. WRENS worked in three watches of eight hours along with the male engineers (also in the Services) who were needed in case of an emergency in the running of the computers. The set-up was that we were given four letter codes which were fed into the machines, which then went through every sequence of the alphabet. This of course took time. If the machine stopped – then Eureka! - you were on to something. The then 'different' four letters were sent to Bletchley by teleprinter. Sometimes you heard of a follow-up but it may be weeks later, everything was so secret, but it gave you a good feeling to know you may have had a hand in moving peace forward. On occasions information could not be used otherwise the Germans would have known that their codes had been broken.

I moved from Steeple Claydon and began living in Woburn Abbey. They had moved much of the valuable furniture and antiques out but there were still some very well-known artworks lodging in the cellars. From Woburn I moved to Wavendon (which became the home of the late Johnny Dankworth and Cleo Laine) whilst still working at Adstock. There were 10,000 men and women working at Bletchley Park from all walks of life. Our backgrounds and educational experiences were wide and varied but we mixed together well and just got on with it. What was remarkable was no one knew what each other did as a job. That was something we never asked.

Although it was wartime, they were happy years. We were well catered for by our officers and we learned not only vital skills to help the war effort but how to live as independent young women. Living near London was a great advantage and much of my time off was spent there. Our capital took an awful beating with air raids and at one point East London suffered raids on 76 consecutive nights. At times it was quite surreal walking around, getting on with your life, while V1s and V2s dropped and no one paid much attention.

On 5th June 1944 it was my day off and I was in Oxford. The skies were black with U.S. bombers, the noise was indescribable and on my return to Woburn the rumours were rife but there was no confirmation until the following day that the Normandy landings had taken place – D Day 6th June.

***Dorothy Freeman** lived in Sheffield at the start of the War and experienced the Sheffield Blitz in 1940. After reading about the First Aid Nursing Yeomanry (FANY), she decided to leave her reserved occupation and enlist.*

Dorothy Freeman – FANY

When I left school at 16 my first job was in administration but by the time I was 21-years-old I was an accountant. It was a reserved occupation and I knew I would never be called up but I read an article about the First Aid Nursing Yeomanry (FANY) and of a woman who belonged to the corps and went horse riding across India. That was the job for me so I applied to enlist and went to London for an interview. The FANY was established in 1899 with the purpose of assisting the Military and Civil Authorities in times of emergency. After being accepted I did my two weeks' training at Bletchley Park. Because of my background in secretarial work and my qualifications they decided this was where my talents would be most useful. The others on my course learned decoding. When my training was over I was sent to Baker Street in London but because of security reasons it was simply known as 98, The Horseguards. I became secretary to the equipment officer. Part of our job was to assist Norwegians who were dropped as secret agents in occupied Europe. I knew a little bit of what was going on but it was highly secret work. I remember one day Odette Sansom coming over to meet me and shake my hand.

Odette Sansom was an allied heroine of World War 11. She was born in Amiens in France but married an

Englishman, Roy Sansom. She worked with the French underground in Nazi occupied France, leaving her three little daughters behind. Eventually she was betrayed and in June 1943 condemned to death in Ravensbruk Concentration Camp. However, she survived and testified at the 1946 War Crimes Tribunal. She was honoured with the George Cross and became an MBE. Later a film was made of her life with Anna Neagle playing Odette.

In July 1945 when the War had moved to the Pacific, I was to be sent to Northern Australia. Unfortunately the injections I had to have made me ill and I never got to go. On V.E. day I was staying in a hostel in St. John's Wood so I cycled over to Buckingham Palace. I stood cheering and waving at the King, Queen, Princesses and Winston Churchill who were standing on the balcony. It was so exciting. There were people everywhere, balancing on lampposts, singing and making merry. I got talking to three American Officers who became worried that I would never get through the crowds back to my digs. So they escorted me back to their place until the mayhem died down. I remember that one of them was into science and showed me some pond life through a microscope. It fascinated me.

I am always amazed now when I think back over 70 years ago, how many of the details I remember as well as the big events.

In 1942 ***Geoffrey Winter*** *left the splendours of a Cambridge college to join the Army. He saw three years of service in Sicily, the Middle East and Germany before* *he was able to return to Cambridge to complete his studies.*

Geoffrey Winter - Army

I was 16-years-old when the War began in September 1939. In August I had returned prematurely from a holiday in France because of the imminence of war, but there was good news for me on my return. In June I had taken the Higher School Certificate examinations and I found that on the strength of my results I had been awarded a State Scholarship and a County Exhibition. Thus the necessary finance for a university education was available. Early in December I travelled by train to Paddington, found my way to Liverpool Street Station in the blackout and arrived in Cambridge in the late evening. There I was interviewed at Corpus Christi College and took the Open Scholarship examination papers which were reckoned to be the most difficult tests a sixth form boy could face. It was also very daunting to negotiate medieval courtyards, corridors and staircases in total darkness.

However, I gained an award and entered Corpus in October 1940 when I was 17. Living accommodation was far better than it is for modern undergraduates. Each of us had a good-sized sitting room, a small pantry and a separate bedroom - but lavatories and baths were a long way off, down flights of stone steps and across the Old Court. There was no hot water supply to the rooms. Each morning the staircase man-servant brought me a jug of hot water, lit the fire (subject to the availability of coal), made the bed and cleared up generally.

Food rationing was in force. The college kitchens did their best but there was an awful lot of bubble and squeak and jugged hare. Breakfast, lunch and dinner were taken in-hall and there was waiter service at all meals. There were times when I was very hungry. Attendance at Training Corps was regular and frequent: I opted for the infantry. At college we had to stay up all night on a rota basis to patrol the premises on fire-watching duty in case of German bombing but we snatched some sleep in bunks in the former bicycle sheds. I completed two academic years at Cambridge when my military service began at the age of 19.

After about seven weeks in the ranks, I was posted to an Officer Cadet Training Unit. I was commissioned in the York and Lancaster Regiment at the end of January 1943 and I was soon put in command of a group of about 20 men to sail to North Africa from where we embarked in landing craft to join the 1st Battalion in Sicily. We joined the Battalion during a battle near the River Simeto and I was put in command of 12 Platoon in B company. Sicily was very hot in July and August and one of my main memories is of being pinned down by German machine gunfire on a very hot day on the solidified lava beds on the slopes of Etna. I survived the campaign, but one of my fellow officers in the company was killed.

After the German withdrawal from Sicily, we crossed the Straits of Messina in landing craft and began our march up the west coast. This was before the Salerno landings and the Italian capitulation. There was just a minor brush with some Germans when I took my platoon on a flanking movement. Further north we moved towards the east and bumped into the Germans near the village of Bonefro. We were being mortared but we got close and I led the platoon in a charge on the German machine-gun positions. Most of the enemy withdrew and we just captured two wounded Germans and four machine guns which might have decimated the company on our left. But this was at the cost of my already under-strength platoon, losing one man killed and seven wounded. All this happened within a very short time - about 15 minutes - illustrating how quickly an infantry unit can be reduced in a very minor action. But this was exemplified more strongly, when after a winter in the mountains and over towards the east coast in snow, rain and mud (infantry men are normally in the open), we were moved near to the west coast to attack the German positions on the River Garigliano. By then I had left 'B' company and had taken over a platoon in 'S' (Support) company.

There are some 400 men in the rifle companies of a battalion and the brunt of the fighting falls on them. In some 48 hours we lost about 300 killed, wounded and missing. While we were holding positions on the Garigliano, I was diagnosed with infective hepatitis and hospitalized. Soon after discharge I went down with malaria and was back in hospital. These illnesses probably saved my life because, while I was away, the Battalion was transferred to the Anzio beachhead which was a hellish place. However, I was fit enough to get to Anzio in time for the attack which led to the breakout preceding the fall of Rome.

By this time, the Battalion was very much in need of a break from action and of reinforcement so we were shipped to the Middle East which meant periods in Palestine, Egypt, Syria (where I helped run a street-fighting school) and Transjordan where we had a lot of fun blowing up pill boxes. We were then sent to France and on to Belgium to prepare for the final assault over the River Elbe into Germany. By then I was in command of a composite platoon of assault pioneers (mines, explosives, manpack flamethrowers) and of a group of heavier flamethrowers mounted on Bren carriers. Across the Elbe we met little resistance and when the War ended we were advancing towards Lübeck.

The atomic bomb on Japan meant I did not have to go to the Far East. Months in various parts of Germany followed. In October I was promoted to be an instructor on the Assault wing of 21 Army Group tactical school but I was offered early release to return to Cambridge. Infantry soldiering in wartime is very different from the study of 18th and 19th century French and German literature (my subjects) but I had to adjust. My brief Army career remains vivid in my memory. Command of 30 or 40 men in action is a tremendous experience for a 20-year-old and I am glad to have had it and to have, against all the odds, emerged unscathed. My regrets have come later; I think that the country now is unworthy of the men who were killed.

*In 1939 **Bessie Renwick** was living in Sheffield and working for the Council in the Transport Department. She was in a reserved occupation but gave this up to join the Auxiliary Territorial Service (ATS). This gave her the opportunity to see different parts of the country which she enjoyed in spite of the hardships of wartime travel.*

Bessie Renwick – ATS

Because I worked for the Transport Dept I was in a reserved occupation but as the War went on the Government asked local authorities to release young women within certain age brackets to join the forces, and so, in 1943, at 22 years of age, I joined the ATS (the women's army). We began with three weeks' training at Pontefract. I really enjoyed this but most girls hated it because there was a lot of PT, route marches and drills which involved a lot of standing and marching in straight lines. I liked the physical activity and have always had a fondness for straight lines.

The only thing that bothered me was that at night we slept in a big barrack room – 60 of us altogether, in bunk beds. When the other girls began talking, they used language I'd never heard before. The swearing was terrible, and they talked about what they did with their boyfriends and what their parents did in bed. I'd never heard anything like it - even using the word 'dash' was regarded as a swear word in our house and not allowed.

I really feared that I would never make any friends in the ATS. Another odd thing to me was that the sergeant would come in at night and inspect under the bedclothes. When I asked why, she told me that many girls were unused to wearing pyjamas and never got undressed for bed at all.

At the end of the three weeks we were all interviewed by an officer and given aptitude tests. It turned out that I was suitable to become an OWL (Operator, Wireless and Line). I was sent to a signals school in Strathpeffer in the Highlands of Scotland which was a lovely part of the world and there I made a good friend. Most of the signals we sent and received were in code, so we didn't know what they were about, but it was work I enjoyed very much. The discipline was strict but quite normal for those times and not irksome.

We moved about the country quite a lot and so I saw parts of the country I would have had no opportunity of doing in my civilian life, as the travel would have cost too much. I particularly enjoyed postings near to Lincoln and York because I loved historical places.

Travel was not exactly easy in wartime because the trains were packed and often delayed. If troop trains were coming through, they would be given priority and the ordinary trains delayed, and air raid damage might cause the train to be diverted. For instance, it took over 23 hours to get from Pontefract to Strathpeffer. There were no refreshments on the trains and getting a seat was almost impossible. Also you didn't know where you were, because all the station signs had been removed. We had to sit on our kitbags in the corridors. In summer you got so hot because you had to wear your big army greatcoat, it being too heavy to carry. It was so crowded you couldn't move and getting to the toilet was almost impossible. Even if you were only going to be away from base for three or four nights, you had to take all your kit with you. Luckily, the other passengers would often be soldiers or other servicemen and they would usually give you a helping hand. You accepted all these discomforts as a fact of life: you were used to it.

It was in the Army that I met my husband, when we were posted to the same place. He later said, "As soon as I saw you, I knew you were the girl I wanted to marry". He had been abroad for most of the War: India, the desert campaign, and even China just before the War. Altogether he was away for six and a half years. That was not uncommon, since most travel was by ship and it took six weeks to get to India. My brother was in the Navy and never saw his child till she was six-years-old.

I was not demobbed until 1946, a year after the War ended and I had to go back to my old job which had been kept open for me.

Rita Brent *loved the time she spent in the Land Army in spite of minor inconveniences like having to find devious ways round the one bath a week allowance, earth closets and frisky lambs.*

Rita Brent – The Land Army

I was 20-years-old when the Second World War began and living in London. Our family home was destroyed in the Blitz and we had nothing left but the clothes we were wearing. I, along with other Londoners, was evacuated by my employer to a hostel in Cirencester, where I took a clerical job. I soon became bored by the lack of stimulation compared with London life and so I joined the Land Army. This appealed to me on two counts. First, I loved the countryside and enjoyed long walks, and second, being a pacifist, I preferred that kind of work to joining the armed forces.

My fiancé, who was also a pacifist, was called up to the Navy and chose to go into minesweepers as this would save lives rather than taking them. He was based initially up at Grimsby and I was sent to an Agricultural College in Somerset for a brief period of training, probably about one month.

My first job after training was on a mixed farm near the village of Fairford in Gloucestershire – lovely countryside, but a complete change from my previous life. The social differences were noticeable. Some farmers had an almost feudal attitude to their workers. They were country people and I was a city girl.

At one farm in Willersley I had to share a bedroom with the daughter of the house, which was not very satisfactory, but at all the other farms I had a bedroom to myself. I never lived in a hostel with other land girls.

The toilets were usually outside. I didn't mind this too much, so long as they were proper water closets but I hated the earth closets. At one farm I had to walk past the sitting room to get to the toilet and the farmer objected to this so I complained to his wife who kindly allowed me to walk through the kitchen instead.

We were only allowed one bath a week and of course we got very dirty and sweaty in our work. I was very fastidious about personal hygiene and directed much of my energies to finding ways round this. Sometimes I got baths at the homes of the Land Army regional organisers and at one farm a neighbour let me use her bathroom. In another village there were a lot of mothers and children evacuated from London, using the village hall to cook in. They also were sympathetic, so one way and another I usually managed three baths a week.

Milking and dairying were my first jobs and looking after all the milking equipment. These had always been the women's tasks on a farm. I loved looking after the cows and calves and helping out with calving, not that I was ever in charge of this, but if an extra hand was needed to pull, I would be there.

In summer the cattle grazed on the hillsides and I would drive them out, sometimes long distances, to find fresh pasture. At Willersey there were many orchards so the patches of grass land were far apart, sometimes several miles. I had a dog to assist me and he was a great help. Although I did not relish getting up at 5.30 or 6.00 a.m., the views over the Vale of Evesham in the early mornings were splendid. It was not so nice in winter and the cattle were kept nearer the farm.

I also looked after the lambs and helped with lambing, then feeding and weaning them and finally taking them to market, but I never took calves to market. The lambs would be frisky on being separated from their mothers, and despite having the help of a dog, I once lost a lamb en route to market. It was run over by an army truck driven by a learner driver. The farmer was furious because he got so much less money for a dead lamb than a live one. I had a fear of heights, so I was not very good climbing ladders to pick the cherry harvest, or on top of the hay carts, one of which I fell off. Realising this, the farmer let me stick to work with the lambs and cows and with the big working horses which pulled the ploughs and carts. I wanted to drive a tractor but never did so. Instead I worked with the horses and took them to the Smithy to be shod. We were able to plough the fields right to the edges and into the corners, unlike using modern tractors.

In addition to the lovely countryside which I enjoyed, I could go shopping in Cheltenham or Gloucester and Stratford-on-Avon was only 15 miles away. The theatre was still open and I managed to get there once: a very long, slow journey by train but I just made it in time for the performance of The Tempest.

One great difficulty I had was seeing my fiancé when he came on leave which was every three months. At

Fairford he was not allowed to come onto the farm, so I moved to a farm at Broadway, where the farmer allowed him to help us in the fields. He was only too glad to have an extra pair of hands. When I was 23 we were married. Our wedding took place in Grimsby and was very simple with two sailors as witnesses and no photographs. Then we had a long train journey, with many changes, to the Lake District for our honeymoon. One rather funny thing was that before I married I was never allowed near the bulls or that side of farm life, but after I was married I had to help.

As I really loved my work and the beautiful Cotswold countryside, the only unhappy aspect of this time for me was the constant fear for the safety of my husband. When I became pregnant I left the Land Army and our daughter was born in June 1945. I really wanted that baby, because if my husband had not returned safely, it would otherwise have felt that I had nothing left of him. Happily he survived, though our daughter was 14-months-old before he saw her as he was out in the Far East.

Despite the tremendous change of lifestyle, I loved the Land Army and wouldn't have missed it for the world.

The Land Army was also ***Patricia Richardson's*** *choice. She joined the forestry branch where she learned to wield axes and cross-cut saws and also acquired a taste for alcohol.*

Patricia Richardson – Land Army

I left school at 16 and was apprenticed into the hairdressing trade but didn't take to it. At 17½ in 1942, but with only the munitions factory on offer locally, I decided to join the Forces. I plumped for the WRENS – simply because I liked the uniform - but they were only recruiting cooks. This was not my forte. So, quite cynically I joined the forestry branch of the Land Army, because they did not work weekends but from 8.00 am – 5.00 pm weekdays.

I ended up being the youngest recruit in the Women's Timber Corps. I wore light brown breeches, a shirt, green tie and sweater, or, when working, brown dungarees. There was an oval badge with crossed axes and fir trees on it. You could have a beret or a felt hat with a brim. I chose the hat to wear as it suited me more. To finish off I had a great coat. It was called a 'bum–freezer' because it only just came below your bottom and the rain ran off it soaking your knees. I was stationed in South Wales in the Mumbles, on an Estate owned by Admiral Heneage-Vivian, cutting timber. There was a sawmill and charcoal kilns but I worked outside on the hillside. I used a 4lb axe and a cross-cut saw.

Initially, I had to complete a six-week training course at Abergorlech working with woodsmen. In a hostel for 30 I was almost the only English girl. Two miles outside the village was a rest camp for soldiers of the Black Watch and we would all meet together in the pub. I had a ball. Here I acquired a taste for alcohol and learned to play dominoes and skittles quite skilfully. The Health and Safety people we hear so much about today would have despaired of us: we used to hitch a lift home sitting astride the top of a water bowser. I made a friend in the village called Glenys and after I finished training I would often go back for weekends. By then the Americans had come to the Rest Camp and we were entertained royally by them.

It was hard work but I was very fit. We were outdoors in all weather so I was also very tanned. The softest wood to chop down was the fir trees but beech was like cutting at an iron post. It could take all day for two of us to fell a large tree. After the trees were felled we trimmed off the branches. Horses or men, depending on the weight of the trunk, pulled them out towards the nearest road and then the tractor took them to the sawmill. The branches were sorted into piles and the thickest were used in the mining industry for pit props and smaller ones, called "cords", were used in the charcoal kilns and eventually for munitions and explosives. The trunks were used as railway sleepers or in the mines except for birch trees. These were carefully selected as they were used in a specialist way – they were sliced very thinly and used to make the outside of aeroplanes.

Sometimes we had to do night shifts on fire-watch in the sawmill. This was because the sawdust became so hot it was a risk. Often we would find grass snakes had crawled into it to warm up. On the odd weekend we girls would work on the single branch line of the railway passing down full-size railway sleepers like pass the parcel. It was all about balance and the way you picked them up. I worked here for about two years until I had a riding accident. After three or four months of sick leave I was told I was now an insurance risk and I had to leave the forestry. I then worked in a menagerie as a Land Girl but looking after parrots and small mammals. I stayed there until the end of the War and I was demobbed.

My years with the Women's Timber Corps were finally rewarded when in 2007 a bronze statue was erected in our honour. It stands in situ in Aberfoyle in the Trossachs National Park and I feel very proud to have been part of the effort that won us the War.

I feel the period I grew up in and the diverse experiences I had during this time gave me a more rounded education in life, people adaptability, and what became history, than I could ever have gained by not being part of it all.

Audrey Ward *joined the Women's Auxiliary Air Force (WAAF) after reading a newspaper advertisement. Initially her feet proved to be a stumbling block to her WAAF career but the problem was solved and she trained as a meteorologist.*

Audrey Ward - WAAF

In late 1941 I read an advertisement in a newspaper for the WAAF which was recruiting women to be trained as meteorologists. This intrigued me as my Geography teacher at school had aroused my interest in the subject. I presented myself at a recruiting centre and, after a medical, waited for a few weeks until I received papers directing me to Innsworth. It was a cold January, and the stoves in our huts did not seem really adequate, but after a week or so we were sent by train to Morecambe. This was just as cold but we were billeted in seaside boarding houses, and, after receiving training in drill, gas mask procedures etc those of us enrolled as 'Mets' were sent to London, where we were billeted in a block of flats near Sloane Square.

This was very exciting for many of us but I had lived in London and so knew my way around. Here I hit a snag. I have long feet (size 9) and the equipment people were unable to provide me with the official shoes. I was summoned to an address in Hallam Street before an officer who asked me: “Are you trying to get your discharge?” I was astonished and assumed I had committed some mysterious Air Force crime. But no, it was just that the shoes did not fit. I had to go round sundry bespoke shoemakers in London to get quotations for my shoes to be specially made.

At the end of the course we were posted all over the place. I was lucky enough to be sent to Plymouth, the Area Combined Headquarters, Western Approaches. It was mainly a Naval station but the Met Office, at that time a civilian organisation, had decided to recruit airwomen as observers/assistants. We were billeted this time in some large houses on the edge of Plymouth, and were bussed in to Mount Wise in eight-hour shifts. We plotted charts, but as we were underground we did not make observations. This was exciting as we had access to the Ops room where a huge wall chart showed the positions of convoys and, with luck, enemy U-boats.

After several months I was posted to Dunkeswell in deepest Devon where life was different. We had squadrons of U.S. Army, Air Force and U.S. Navy at different times and U.S. rations. We hadn't seen fruit salad for years. One thing dismayed us about the Americans: there were black soldiers as well as white ones, but the black soldiers had to line up outside the mess hall and wait until the white soldiers had finished their meal before they were allowed to eat. Met was arguably one of the best trades in the WAAF. The Met Office on an RAF station was adjacent to the Ops room so we knew what was going on. On each shift there would be a forecaster and a couple of WAAFs as observers and plotters. We made an observation of the weather (temperature, humidity, pressure etc) every three hours. This info was then coded into five-digit groups and transmitted by teleprinter to ETA (the code name for the Met Office which we later discovered was at Dunstable). The messages for the whole country were then transmitted back to every Met Office, whereupon the Met WAAFs would grab it and proceed to plot the situation at every reporting station on a blank chart.

Plotting involved seizing our plotting pens, one red and one black, which were lashed together so that we could move from one colour to another without having to pick up different pens. For instance, temperature and pressure were in black and visibility in red. When we had finished the whole country, the chart would be passed to the forecaster who would draw the isobars and the weather fronts.

Life in the Met Office was usually relaxed and friendly, though it could be stressful when operations needed certain weather conditions which failed to materialize.

At first the forecasters were civilians, but in (I think) 1943 they suddenly appeared in uniform as Flying Officers and Flight Lieutenants. Later on in the War a new breed of Met observers appeared: young men from the Commonwealth who were exotic because they were black. It was a matter of some amusement that they were never allowed to do night duty and so they would cheerily say goodnight at 22:00 hours and go off duty while we had to continue on through the night.

I was fortunate, having been posted to Coastal Command, that the stations where I was based did not experience the awful casualties of Bomber and Fighter stations. At Limavady I found myself in charge of gramophone concerts - much appreciated. The sets of records had to be changed at ENSA HQ in Belfast. They were too heavy for me to carry, but one day a kind Fleet Air Arm Petty Officer from 825 Squadron, temporarily based at Limavady, offered to take them and choose a new set. (Reader, I married him.)

Towards the end of the War we realised that we Met WAAFs would soon be scattered to the four winds and never see each other again. So was formed the Ex Metwaaf Association - EMWA. We contacted every Met

Office via the teleprinter network and for years afterwards met for dinners, lunches and visits to such places as Kew Gardens, Linton-on-Ouse RAF Station, and the spanking new Met Office at Exeter.

*With a brother in the Canadian Air Force and a sister in the WAAF, **Beryl Harrison** was keen to do her bit even though she was in a reserved occupation. She became a wireless operator in the WAAF and volunteered to go to Germany at the end of the War.*

Beryl Harrison – WAAF

Although I was in a reserved occupation in Sheffield, I volunteered for the WAAF when I was seventeen and a half, and began training as soon as I was eighteen in September 1942. My older sister was already in the WAAF and my brother was a pilot in the Royal Canadian Air Force, so I was keen to do my bit.

My first week was at a WAAF station in Gloucester, when we had medicals and were kitted out, and from there we went to Morecambe for three weeks' initial training. We used to have lectures on the pier, marching there and back, but being given the order 'break step' once we got on to the pier, lest our marching should cause the pier to collapse! My rank at entry was Aircraftwoman 2 (ACW2). At Morecambe we went on Church Parade with the RAF, and I wrote enthusiastically to my mother – 'it was the first time I marched to a band and, boy, did I like it!'

I was waiting for a place on the teleprinter course at Cranwell, and meantime was sent to RAF Cottesmore in Rutland, where we lived in a big country house that had been requisitioned by the Government for the use of WAAF personnel. I was put into the Signal Section. We had three crashes here in the space of three nights because there had been a lot of night flying. I had to send telegrams with bad news. One was to the Air Ministry arranging for the funeral of one of our American pilots who had been killed, and the other informing the wife of a Canadian of his death in the same crash.

The course at Cranwell lasted 12 weeks. I arrived in December – it was bitterly cold and at one point the pipes froze, meaning no baths. To get more teleprinter operators trained than would otherwise have been the case, our intake was split into two, one half studying from 6am – 2pm, the other from 2pm – 10pm. Because I had done well in the exams, I was chosen to be flight leader and we were on the 6am – 2pm shift. The girls were billeted in what had been the married quarters and which were fairly well spread out. I was awakened in the mornings at 4.30am by the duty sergeant, who shone a torch in my face to wake me, and then thrust a book at me to sign. I would put on my greatcoat over my thick winceyette pyjamas, then my hat, gloves and scarf and go out into the snow to wake up the thirty-odd other girls. Then we would march in the pitch dark, with one hurricane lamp carried at the front, and another by a girl at the back. Our first call was at the cookhouse where we were given mugs of strong, hot, sweet tea and a slice of fruitcake. Then we marched to our classes. When our first class of the day was teleprinting we found it difficult as our hands were numb with cold. Other lectures we had were on procedure and teleprinter maintenance. At 9am we marched to the cookhouse for a proper cooked breakfast. We were well fed with porridge followed by a cooked meal. The toast, butter and marmalade being put on the same plate as the eggs and bacon.

Although we had very little spare time, the leisure facilities at Cranwell were excellent, including dramatic societies, films, ENSA concerts, dancing classes and many other things. There was also a gymnasium and a heated swimming pool and I sent home for my swimsuit. We were invited to tea by the padre one day. There was no hot water in the married quarters when the water froze, but we could send clothes to the laundry. I passed out from the course as ACW1.

My next posting was to Fighter Command Telecommunication Flying Unit at Defford in Worcestershire. The Telecommunication Research Establishment was at Malvern, about 8 miles away, and both were secret stations because they were dealing with the research and installation of radar equipment. Planes of all kinds flew into Defford to have this equipment installed. Flight testing of the equipment took place at Defford. It was all very interesting and I enjoyed being there. The station covered a big area and we were issued with cycles in order to get around. We teleprinter operators in the Signal Section worked a three shift system with morning, afternoon and night duties. After night duty we had the next day off. We used to sleep for a few hours and then get on our bikes and cycle out into the countryside.

It was a lovely summer and one day my friend Elsie and I, who had been on night watch together, decided to cycle to Stratford-on-Avon, and to put our bikes on the train for the return journey. Alas, when we got there we found that no train was running, so after a quick snack in a teashop, we cycled back to Defford, doing about 70 miles in that one day. It meant that we were late back as we had not applied for late passes (after 10pm) so we were both put on a charge. This led to seven days 'jankers', i.e. extra duties, such as scrubbing floors, peeling potatoes etc. Once I had to clean out a huge porringer!

One day I had cycled to meet Betty, a friend of mine from Sheffield, also in the WAAF, who was stationed at Gloucester. I got back after dark entering the aerodrome by a different gate than usual. The duty sergeant on the gate told me that because I did not have a light on my bike I would have to get off and push, (getting batteries was a problem during the War). It was such a vast airfield and in complete darkness that I did not really know where I was, but suddenly I heard a noise behind me. I looked up to see that I was under a big Lancaster bomber coming in to land – I had strayed onto a runway!

In the Signal Section, I could hear the wireless operators at work in the next room and I thought it sounded exciting, so I applied to go on the wireless operator course. In June 1944 I was posted to Blackpool to do the first half of the six month course. Travelling in wartime could be difficult, and the journey to Blackpool by train took nine hours and involved four changes. We were billeted in requisitioned boarding houses and our landladies did not feed us very well – they would have preferred holidaymakers, I am sure, and food was in short supply of course. The result was that we spent a good deal of money on fish and chips! On one memorable occasion, I had taken a friend home with me for our weekend leave, Sheffield being nearer than where she lived in London. When we got back to our boarding house, we found that one of our rooms had been let to holidaymakers, and we had to share a bed for several days. I learnt then that Stella ground her teeth when asleep!

Blackpool was absolutely packed with RAF and WAAF personnel. We took over the Tower Ballroom and the Winter Gardens for lectures. It was in the Tower Ballroom that dozens of WAAF sat in rows at long benches receiving Morse being sent by an RAF NCO who sat at the front on a high platform. These morse transmissions were speeded up as we progressed, and later interference was added. The phrase 'going for a burton' derives from Blackpool. Burton's men's outfitters was where we went for tests. It was located on a very windy corner. Once we had a march past to celebrate the WAAF birthday. Together with the RAF we marched all over Blackpool with two bands, but it was so windy that we had to wear chin straps to keep our hats from blowing off. Several had blown off before these commands were given. 'Parade halt. WAAF remove hats.

WAAF adjust straps. WAAF replace caps. Parade by the left quick march!' We could hardly hear the orders because of the wind and the deafening roar of the sea, and these were the strangest orders we had ever heard!

After the first three months we were moved to RAF Compton Basset near Swindon, to complete the course. It was a big station with 5,000 personnel, including two Jamaican squadrons. We continued with lessons in procedure, technical and the sending and receiving of Morse. Technical lessons involved learning about motor generators, transformers and field telephones. I preferred being based in a camp rather than civilian billets. My brother was stationed fairly near, and had a red sports car and once or twice came to take me for a spin.

After the course, I was posted, in December 1944, to Plymouth as Leading Aircraftwoman (LACW) wireless operator, and we were accommodated in a large house on Tavistock Road. The centre of the city had been badly bombed, and we very rarely went there. WAAF were not allowed to go on Union Street, but one afternoon my friend, Joan and I, were invited by two American Navy friends to go to a café there for a steak and chips meal. This was a real treat and off we went. The café was upstairs and our meal arrived, but suddenly there was a noise and some other sailors began fighting. Our hosts got us out of there fast, leaving the lovely steak and chips half eaten. There were many different navies in Plymouth: French, Norwegian, Polish, etc. and of course, American. Squabbles and fights often broke out between them. I was too innocent to realize it, but I think that Union Street was probably the red light district, and that is why we were forbidden to go there. I have a lovely memory of Union Street though, and that is going on Church Parade there, with RAF and WAAF marching and being led by the wonderful Royal Marine band.

We worked underground at Mount Wise in Plymouth, the RAF together with the Navy. Our signal section had sets linked to the Azores and to Gibraltar also Air Sea Rescue sets and listening out sets. We had watches every third night. One night I was on the listening out set, which could be boring and I feared I might fall asleep, but I picked up a very faint emergency signal. The atmospherics meant that I only caught part of the message, but it included our call sign. Usually the other stations in our group would come up acknowledging receipt of a message, but nobody else was answering. I followed usual procedure and pressed the red light at my side to show that I had received a message. The NCO took the message, returning shortly afterwards with the reply that I had to transmit, and accompanied by two high ranking officers. I sent the reply and was now getting much clearer reception from the sender and the rest of the group were acknowledging receipt. All ended well. The pilot of the aircraft, somewhere abroad, was either lost or running out of fuel and our messages had given him instructions where to land. As in teleprinting, all signals were sent in code with very few in 'plain language'. On this occasion, I got to hear of the outcome.

I was in Plymouth when the war in Europe ended and on VE Day everyone went up on to the Hoe to celebrate. Bonfires were lit, and I think it was the Americans who pulled up wooden benches to stoke them! Searchlights criss-crossed the sky, ships were lit up with what looked like fairy lights, their sirens sounded and everyone was singing and dancing. It was a fantastic night, but I don't recall being late back to Trevorlick, (our hostel), as we were tired out with all the excitement.

At the end of August, 1945 I was at RAF Snailwell, near Newmarket. We were to be trained as telephone operators, but it didn't happen in the end. Instead, I was doing clerical work. Newmarket was a lovely place to be. From the bottom of the garden at Amberley House, where we were living, you could get straight on to the Heath where the racehorses trained. Each morning and again at 4pm we would see them pass the side of the house on their way to gallop on the Heath. One day we went to the races and one of the horses I backed came in first. I spent the winnings celebrating my 21st birthday with my friends. As Snailwell was the Belgian Training School there were more Belgians than English at the station. These were men who had escaped from occupied Belgium via the Pyrenees and come to England to join the fight. There was more fraternising – they were all nice and good company and my French improved greatly. Some of the Belgians spoke Flemish though, and they and the French-speakers did not always get on well.

Finally, I volunteered to go to Germany. Our train journey through the Ruhr showed the awful extent of the bombing and when the train slowed down the children would come begging for food. We gave them what we had. I spent nearly a year there at Bűckeburg, in Westphalia before I was demobbed in 1947.

Don Kelly *tells us his own and his brother* ***Bernard's*** *story. Both were in the Royal Air Force (RAF) but Bernard was captured by the Germans in 1941 and became a prisoner of war. Don trained as a ground wireless operator but later retrained under the Pilot, Navigator, Bomb-aimer scheme and flew on bombing missions.*

Don Kelly and Bernard Kelly – RAF

In the late summer of 1939 I was a young boy who played cricket for the "Derby Evening Telegraph". We had a fixture with "The Cheltenham Echo", played away on a Sunday in Gloucester. My older brother, Bernard, also played and found himself chatting to one of our tail-enders, a printer by the name of Pat Moore.

War was declared on 3rd September. Bernard enlisted in the RAF at Cardington, came home for a few days and then, after telling us he had been selected for pilot training, disappeared for a long time as he began his long course.

In June 1940, being young and foolish, I went to Cardington and joined up to be trained as a ground wireless operator. After being kitted out with uniform and enduring two or three weeks' drill training in Morecambe, I was sent to RAF Kinloss in northern Scotland where I did odd jobs and waited for my wireless operator course to begin.

The first posting for the wireless course was in the centre of Liverpool. Our classrooms were in the Liverpool Post Office and our instructors were P.O. employees who had been wireless operators in World War One. Apart from frequent bombing around us, I found Liverpool a pleasant place to live in.

Eventually this part of our course was completed and before we left we arranged a farewell party in the city. While we were imbibing in the hotel, a massive air raid had been taking place outside. A friend, Stan Sly, and I staggered out into a large paved square in the city centre. The ack ack guns were blazing and the spent pieces of flak were raining down on the paving stones causing sparks to fly up. Stan looked at this lot and shouted: "Look, pretty lights!"

We shuffled back to our billets, walking on broken glass for hundreds of yards at a time and seeing the odd bomb dropping nearby. We did not have helmets but we reached our billets unscathed.

We then left Liverpool and moved on to finish our course at RAF Cranwell. We arrived in darkness and the barrier was lifted by a fellow who quoted as we filed in: "Abandon hope all ye who enter here!" There were two camps, East Camp where wireless people were trained and West Camp where pilots were trained.

During our course in Cranwell we were forced to learn drill. Having spent some time drilling as a new recruit, I had no objection to it but I had every objection to the Acting Corporal who carried out the duty, for he was universally detested, so three of us decided to take action. We found out where the Acting Corporal's billet was and one night, half an hour or so after lights out, we slipped out. We trotted round to our 'friend's' billet, lifted up the window, pulled back the black-out curtains, and emptied the contents of a large fire bucket over the sleeping Acting Corporal's bed. We ran back to our billet, closed the window and went back to bed. Nothing was heard of the matter and the Acting Corporal disappeared.

One morning in early 1941 I was called to our administrative sergeant's office. Wondering what I had done wrong, I entered the office and there, sitting side by side were Bernard, replete with his pilot's wings, and none other than my printer friend, Pat Moore.

Bernard had completed his pilot training and had been posted to a Bomber Operational Training Unit where he learned to fly the Vickers Wellington bomber. When this was completed he went to a large hangar where pilots, navigators, wireless operators and gunners were gathered. There they mingled and were free to select who they would crew up with. Pat and Bernard remembered meeting before and they elected to crew up together.

We had a good chat but before he left Bernard took me to one side and asked me if I had volunteered to take an air-gunners' course after finishing my wireless operators' course. I confessed that I had. Bernard then spoke to me seriously and pointed out a few facts. As a flying wireless operator I would see nothing other than the set and for long hours would simply be listening out. He advised me to drop it. I did and this probably saved my life. At the end of the War, it was revealed that 50 per cent of Bomber Command were either killed or became prisoners of war.

Cranwell was not far from my home in Derby and at weekends I frequently went home to see my mother who was now alone after bringing up a family of seven, my father having died 10 years previously. At the end of March I went home to find that mother had received the dreaded telegram: "Regret to tell you that your son, Sergeant-Pilot Bernard Kelly, is missing after a raid in Germany".

The following week she received two contradictory letters from Wyton where Bernard was stationed. One was from the station Padre who said that she must accept that her son had not survived as a burning aircraft had been spotted near his target that night. The other, from the Station Commanding Officer, said that he had no news as yet, but would communicate with her as soon as he had anything to report.

The contradictory reports of the two letters puzzled me and I determined to find the reason for this so I applied for compassionate leave. This was not approved so I collected a haversack, put in a towel and toilet items and hitch-hiked to Wyton to sort it out.

I made my way to the guard room and told the guard on sentry duty why I had come. Within minutes I was facing the officer commanding RAF Wyton. He asked why I had come and I explained about the contradictory letters received by my mother. To my great relief he said: "You have done the right thing. Padre has got it wrong and as yet I have no news. As soon as I have any, I will contact your mother".

He was very friendly so I confessed that I had come without permission and told him what had happened. He just nodded and I left. Thinking that I might as well be hung for a sheep as a lamb, I went to see my oldest sister who lived near St Alban's to give her my news. I returned to Cranwell two days later and, although I had been absent without leave, I never heard a word about it. I can only imagine that RAF Wyton had been in contact with them. About two weeks later I received a telegram from my mother: "Bernard alive. A prisoner of war".

Our wireless operators' course finished and I was posted to 231 Squadron, an Army Co-operation squadron working with the Army in Northern Ireland. Northern Ireland was used as a training ground for the Army and it was our job to accompany them on manoeuvres with a van containing radio equipment. We received messages from our pilots and transferred them to our airfield at Newtownards, near Belfast. Sometimes the pilots would manually send messages directly to the Army by wrapping the message in a container which they dropped from the plane in a small fabric bag with a long tail which could be seen when dropped, fluttering to the ground.

While I was with 231 Squadron we had two fully-blown inspections: the first was by the RAF officer in charge of the Airforce in Northern Ireland, but the second was by the King, George VI. We stood to attention in ranks as the King walked by, followed by the Queen (who later became the Queen Mother). I thought King George looked ill but I was most impressed by the Queen. It seemed to me that as she walked along our ranks she had time to smile at each man as she passed.

In 1942 there were plans for a great expansion of the RAF. Airmen could volunteer to join what was called the Pilot, Navigator, Bomb-aimer (PNB) Scheme. If they could pass a strict physical test and had the necessary educational standard, they could be trained as a pilot, navigator or bomb-aimer. I put in an application for this scheme. There were just two from the whole squadron who were accepted.

We were posted to the Aircrew Receiving Centre in London, kitted out with flying gear and then sent to an Initial Training Wing in Newquay, Cornwall. Here we were trained in basic navigation, meteorology and aircraft recognition and there was plenty of physical training.

After final tests and exams, we were sent out to experience flying. I was sent to a place called Booker, near High Wycombe, where Tiger Moths were flown. It was too windy for any of us to fly solo but it was our first experience of flying.

We were sent to Manchester where a big aircrew receiving centre was stationed. The PNB trainees were then to be transported to one of three places: South Africa, USA or Canada: ideal places to train aircrew, having space, decent climate – and no blackout to contend with. We went to Greenock to board the liner which was taking us to Canada. Once on board we found out we had other troops to accompany us, namely German POWs from Rommel's Afrika Corps. As they came aboard they all made a quick dive to grab a life jacket, most probably with U-Boats in mind.

The POWs were in a large cage down below. One night I was on sentry duty down there. We were ordered not to have any contact with them but I took a risk. I thought of Bernard in Germany, relying on Red Cross parcels, and when I felt that the Army sergeant in charge was not looking, I pulled out a large block of chocolate I had bought at the canteen and held it behind me near their cage. It was gone in a flash.

On arrival in Canada, we were sent to a training centre for wireless navigators by the shores of Lake Huron. At the end of the course those who passed it were offered a choice between joining Coastal Command in N.E.

Canada or going to Nova Scotia where a Mosquito Aircraft Course was held. I chose the latter place.

I crewed up with a Canadian, Stuart Johnson, known as "Johnny". The course took place and there were two fatalities on it. When the course was finished we were shipped back to England to complete our final Operational Unit. There was much to learn and we were now flying in a real blackout and in a war zone, but we managed it.

Johnny and I were posted to an operational squadron stationed at RAF Hunsdon, just north of London. This squadron flew the Mosquito fighter-bomber, equipped with four machine guns, four cannons and bombs. They operated at night, usually from a height of 3000 feet. After three days' training we were ready for operations and in September, 1944, we began. Our first flight was to patrol an area of North-East Germany and Northern Holland. When returning we were a little to starboard of our track and flew over Emden Bay where we experienced furious anti-aircraft fire aided by search lights. It was then that I remembered the excellent advice from instructors in Canada, ex-operational navigators. They pointed out that if a searchlight swept towards your plane, don't run away from it, fly towards it and through it. Johnny flew on instruments and I directed him using this advice. In no time we were in the clear, leaving behind a hot-bed of anti-aircraft fire.

Johnny and I then became part of the squadron, flying the type of operations they were involved with at that time. Sometimes we were given definite targets: airfields and troop concentrations in particular, but often it was a case of attack what you could see. Flying in complete blackness at 3000 feet you could not see a lot, but such things as trains could be identified by the plume of smoke rising while mechanical transport gave themselves away by showing lights. We had by this time left Fighter Command and joined the Second Tactical Airforce. We moved from Hunsdon to Hertford Bridge, south-west of London, for a period of training which included low-level bombing and dive-bombing.

In December we flew a mission to the Ardennes to prevent the Germans achieving their object of reaching Rotterdam and the Channel. To begin with things went well. The sky was clear with some moonlight but it was bitterly cold. As we crossed the sea we heard on the intercom that several of our crews had lost instruments from pito-heads icing up and had returned to base. But it was beautifully clear and Johnny could fly with ease without instruments, so we decided to keep going. We had been given a precise target using the G-Box and eventually reached our bombing run. And ran into cloud. Suddenly we were blind and groping our way in a mist, Johnny having nothing but the seat of his pants to fly with. I then heard him say, quite normally: “We’ve had it now”. I found myself babbling incoherently: “Fly on what you’ve got Johnny”. I then realised that we were nose down and plummeting to earth. Then the factors which had caused our problems saved us. We broke cloud, diving vertically down. The ground was covered with snow which Johnny could see – he pulled the stick back hard. Later, much later, he told me that we pulled out of the dive so violently that he ricked his back. We were now in pale moonlight again and, with a full load of bombs, we made our way back, the American Army firing at us as we left.

The Tactical Airforce was now free to attack the German infiltration into the Ardennes. This was probably the last time that the German Army went on the offensive in Europe but the USA and British Armies eventually halted it. We played our part bombing and using our cannons in night-time raids.

One afternoon at Hunsdon a few of us were standing by our aircraft in a bay near the end of the runway when one of our planes, practising landing on one engine, overshot and went crashing through the shrubbery. Leading the chase, I jumped over an RAF Regiment gunpit containing startled men who had just had an aircraft bounce over them. The plane came to a halt and began to burn fiercely, but the pilot and navigator got out in time.

Once we flew on a daylight formation operation: not the type of flying we had been trained for. We were at the rear of the squadron and as we encountered heavy turbulence, I saw debris fly up from the tail of one of our aircraft as the plane behind it made contact. Incredibly, both planes made it back, one on one engine and the other with a badly damaged rudder. We flew low over the Dutch islands and I was thrilled to see Dutch children waving to us. We then broke formation as each of us had our own target, a railway junction or station. We dropped two 500 lb bombs with a delayed action, otherwise we would have gone up with them. On this flight we had a new C.O., strangely an English pilot. He failed to return but we heard later somehow, that he and his navigator were safe: probably picked up by the Dutch Underground.

In March the Squadron moved over to the Continent, to Coxyde, near the Belgian border, a few miles to the east of Dunkirk. The German Army was still in Dunkirk, but completely cut off. We did not have much trouble with them when we were flying, but they managed to shell the airfield. From Coxyde we attacked the German Army as they retreated and in April the Squadron moved into Holland, to a place called Volkel, south of Amsterdam. And here, on 19th April 1945, we finished our Tour of 51 Operations, still in one piece.

The War was winding to a close but while in Volkel Johnny and I took part in a most illegal flight. Johnny was friendly with one of our ground crew, a Sergeant Ericcson, who had never known his father, as he had been killed in WW1. Ericcson knew where his father was buried but had never had the chance to see the grave. Johnny wangled a flight to Epinoy in Belgium, near the WW1 cemeteries. But how to get Ericcson there? A Mosquito was a tight fit for two and he was about six feet tall. He produced a tool box, placed it between my feet and sat on it. It was crowded, highly illegal, but it worked and Ericcson got to see his father's grave.

This was the end of the War for me. Johnny went back to Canada and after a time rejoined the Royal Canadian Air Force. I stayed in the RAF until 1946 while making up my mind as to what to do with my future.

Bernard's Story

In May, 1945, and in the middle of the night, Bernard returned to Derby. By coincidence I happened to be home and he then related to me the events of that night in late March 1941, and the subsequent years.

Bernard had completed his pilot training and was posted to a Bomber Operational Training Unit where he learned to fly the Wellington Bomber. One night in late March 1941 his Squadron was sent on a night raid to Bremen in North-West Germany. After crossing the Dutch-German border the plane was picked up and coned by searchlights. His speed would have been about 120 mph and his height 8,000 to 10,000 feet. Suddenly the flak started but they were not hit. And then the flak abruptly stopped. Bernard called out over the intercom: "Look out for fighters!" As he spoke, the first of a stream of tracer bullets flew down the length of the fuselage. The plane was badly damaged and he lost the use of one engine, but lost the fighter plane on his tail. His navigator was badly wounded but they were still airborne and Bernard turned the stricken plane back the way they had come.

When they reached the German-Dutch border he knew they could not continue and looked for a place they could crash land. Eventually he saw something glinting in a straight line which he took to be a road. He managed to manoeuvre the damaged aircraft along this straight area and made a perfect landing. It was not a road. They had landed on a railway line! Pilot Officer McCoy, the navigator, was badly hurt. They opened up a parachute and, using it as a stretcher, managed to carry him out of the plane and laid him down on the rail line by the crashed aircraft. Bernard then went to the rear of the plane and opened the air-gunner's turret, had one look, and closed it. The second pilot had a minor injury and it appeared that Bernard and Pat Moore were the only crew members who were unhurt.

On the farther side of the track Bernard saw a hut containing a foreign worker who had a small lantern. He motioned to the worker that he wanted to use it. With the lantern in his hand, he walked off down the track. A train was travelling towards him and he waved the lantern and the train came to a halt. The engine crew and passengers came out on to the track and were apparently not very pleased to see that they had been stopped by a British airman. However, their mood changed when they saw the crashed aircraft on the line and realised what would have happened if they had not stopped. The civilian police arrested the crew and prepared to take them away. Some nuns arrived and took P.O. McCoy away with them. Bernard was told later that his navigator had died.

The crew were about to be taken away by the police when a Luftwaffe officer drove up, pulled his rank over the police and took over. He then beckoned Bernard and Pat to get into his car and drove off into the night. They entered a forest and the car stopped. The German officer told the two to get out. Pat Moore later told me that he thought that the German was going to shoot them. He was not, but simply asked if they wanted to have a pee. They continued their journey and eventually arrived at an aerodrome and found themselves face to face with a German pilot. He was none other than the night-fighter pilot who had shot them down. Pat told me that he did not like the look of the man but Bernard had a conversation with him and in fact they both gave each other their home addresses. By the Geneva Convention Bernard and Pat were not obliged to give any military information, just their name, rank and number. They then were taken away to become prisoners of war, but later Bernard was to hear news of this German fighter-pilot.

They were both sent to a prisoner of war camp containing many airmen. The camp commandant then sent for Bernard and told him that he had something for him: a bottle of whisky. It appeared that the head of the Luftwaffe, Herman Goering, had been told of the British airman who had landed his crippled plane safely on a railway line. Whether it was because of his skill in doing this or the fact that a crash with the train had been prevented, Goering, a World War One pilot, had decided to acknowledge it with the whisky. Bernard refused to accept the whisky: no collaborating with the enemy. Bernard and Pat were moved to several POW camps to the east and at each camp the new Camp Commandant called Bernard in to offer him his whisky and each time it was refused. For four years they were prisoners. In the spring of 1945 Bernard was called in for his whisky. This was again refused, but this time the Commandant said to him: “Look, if you don’t take it, they will!” and he pointed to the east where the rumble of the approaching Russian Army could be heard. So the whisky was finally accepted and consumed by Bernard and Pat.

Streams of civilians were now moving westward past the camp and it was decided by the Germans that the POWs were to leave the camp and, under the guard of soldiers, would march in the same direction. For many days they marched and with the little food they were given it was a great hardship. Eventually, when they were resting by the roadside, Bernard motioned to Pat and they both rolled back into the ditch behind them. The march then continued without them. Eventually they saw a British Army scout car, made contact and were free.

They were taken back, given hospital treatment and then sent back to England. After a period of leave Pat went back to his job as a printer and Bernard stayed in the RAF. He began by working as a flying instructor and then, in 1947, was involved in the Berlin Airlift. Berlin was blockaded by the East Germans and for a time the only way they could receive food was by air.

Bernard got to know that the pilot who shot him down had been killed but his widow was still alive in Berlin. He decided to take food to her and her family while he was in Berlin and asked my mother if she could arrange a food parcel for him to take. She sent the parcel to Bernard but he was prevented from delivering it. He was quite bitter about it.

After the War, Bernard began to fly helicopters. He worked on Christmas Island where the British were testing a nuclear bomb. He became ill and eventually retired from the RAF. He died in 1977.

At the age of 18, and against her father's wishes, ***Norma Falk*** *joined the Red Cross as a Voluntary Aid Detachment (VAD) attached to the Army Medical Corps. Hoping to see the world, she was disappointed to find her first posting was in Sheffield, her home city. She volunteered to go abroad at the end of the War and was sent to Germany where she heard of the horrors that had taken place during the War as a nurse at the Lüneberg War Crimes Tribunal.*

Norma Falk – Red Cross Nurse

I was still at school when the War started, and living in Sheffield. We were evacuated for a while, and then when I left school I went to Commercial College and did a few clerical jobs. When I was about 18 I decided to volunteer for nursing with the Red Cross as a VAD (Voluntary Aid Detachment) but when I came home and told my father what I'd done, he was horrified. "It's so unladylike," he said, but I went anyway.

Amazingly there was a waiting list to join, about eight months long, but then we were trained in First Aid and Home Nursing. Miss Connell, the Red Cross Commandant, arranged for me to work at a small miners' hospital at Denaby Main. There were only three wards and no resident doctor. When the accidents came in every night, we sent for the local doctor. Matron would come downstairs in her dressing gown, putting on her white cuffs as she walked, and made the patients comfortable before the doctor saw them.

We had eggs for breakfast every morning because Matron kept chickens, and when we were on night duty, the maids brought us a tray of tea. It was quite unlike any ordinary hospital. The height of excitement for us was a visit to the pictures in Denaby.

We were attached to the Army Medical Corps, going first to a reception camp in York where we were billeted in old houses. It was freezing cold at night. From there we were posted to different hospitals around the country. I couldn't believe it when my posting came – it was to Sheffield – and I'd joined up to see the world. We were at an army reception station where soldiers came with mundane problems like sore throats, and we lived with the other nurses in a house on Gladstone Road. One of our jobs there was to make the beds. We often found gin bottles underneath the bed of one of the sisters, who was a Q.A. (Queen Alexandra's Royal Nursing Corps). The Medical Officer was a heavy drinker and was always tipsy on sick parade.

From there I did an Army Blood Transfusion Course in Bristol and was there at the end of the War, when I volunteered to go abroad. We were sent to Germany in July 1945, and still had to take our gas masks. We assembled at Boyce Barracks, Aldershot, where we were supplied with khaki trousers and battledress to replace our navy uniforms. We spent one night in Brussels en route, sleeping in a hospital, and then a large Dakota transport plane flew us to Germany. Forty nurses went out, and half of us were sent to Lüneberg, where we were billeted in an old barracks, which we tried to make comfy. We took our baths communally in a row of tin tubs, until we managed to put up some curtains for privacy, and we washed at long troughs of cold water. Whenever we went out we had to have an Army escort, because there were still snipers in the forest, and they had to sign us in and out.

The Lüneberg War Crimes Trials

These were the first War crimes trials, before the one at Nuremberg, and the accused had all worked at the Belsen Concentration Camp. They included Kramer, the Commandant, and the camp doctor, Klein, plus several women guards. The trial lasted about two months. Both the prosecution and the defence lawyers were British officers, so it was a slow business because they needed interpreters to translate every question and answer. My duty was to provide minor medical attention to the women prisoners, providing aspirins, escorting them between the dock and the witness box and sitting with them during questioning, in case they fainted. As they spoke no English and I, no German, we had no conversations.

As the trials proceeded and the long catalogue of horror and tragedy unfolded, I was shocked by the complacency and lack of remorse shown by most of the accused. The commandant of Belsen, Kramer, sat impassively throughout, scribbling notes. Klein, the camp doctor, who was accused of conducting experiments on the helpless humans under his care, most of whom died, showed little or no regret at the debasement and prostitution of his medical skill. Although some of the prisoners were clearly thugs, many, especially the women, seemed like ordinary people from ordinary homes.

Irma Grese, 21-years-old and blonde, was one of the most dreaded wardresses of Belsen, and remained unmoved as she heard herself described as The Beast of Belsen. She had beaten many prisoners to death, become adept at torture and even killed babies, yet all trace of pity or compassion was absent. She smiled and posed for the press photographers as if she was a star.

Another woman, Juana Borman, was also adept at torture and used to set dogs on the prisoners. She sat sullen and still during her trial, showing no feeling. Both these women and most of the other accused were hanged, and they knew that would be their fate. All showed a similar lack of human emotion, remorse or regret, even when faced with the pitiable survivors whose evidence was so heartrending. I was only 21-years-old and was pretty shaken. When questioned, the answer they all gave was "Das ist nicht wahr" (that is not true) or "Das had' nicht gesehen" (I did not see that). I was there when Colonel Backhouse donned his black cap and pronounced the death sentences. The prisoners showed no emotion whatsoever, knowing that this was bound to happen.

Years later, my teenage granddaughter asked me: "How could you give aspirins and care to those wicked women?" I said that I was in the Army and under orders, that it was my duty, and she replied: "But that's what the Germans said". I explained that they had to have a fair trial, and I think she eventually understood.

We did visit Belsen, much of which had been pulled down, but the camp hospital was still there as it was just outside the main camp. Our Colonel was so horrified by what he saw that he told us on no account must we give spare food to the German women who worked in our accommodation – it must go for pig swill. Nevertheless, we did sometimes give them food because they were starving.

After the trials I was posted to a proper hospital in Hamburg. There were 20 of us, and we worked hard. Though I was not a fully-trained nurse I performed most of the duties, gave injections etc. I hated the medical wards, especially the skin ward. The men were very rough. One day, despite trembling with fear, I asked a patient to clear some dirty old crusts off the ward table, and he just swept them onto the floor. However, after a few weeks they became quiet like lambs. Hamburg was a pleasanter place to live. Despite the bomb damage they had restored part of the Opera House and we were given tickets for it, which began my love of opera. There were also concerts to attend.

In 1948 I was demobbed, and whilst servicemen were given 'demob suits', we women were given a small cash allowance to buy civilian clothes.

Some years ago, my grandson bought me a book which contained an exact transcript of the Lüneberg trials, and as I read the questions and answers, I could see each prisoner clearly in my mind's eye. Some of my accounts and experiences have been filmed by the Spielberg Institute in the U.S.A. and the Holocaust Memorial Centre near Ollerton in Nottinghamshire has photographs.
Man's inhumanity to man – will we ever learn?

Holocaust Survivors

These three stories present a harrowing and moving picture of life for Jews in countries under Nazi control. We see the bewilderment of children suddenly realising that they were 'different', but not knowing why, lives turned upside down and families parted, some never to meet again. We see both the best and the worst of human nature.

***Rolf Heymann**, living in Germany, describes his terror during Kristallnacht (Night of the Broken Glass), when Jewish homes, shops and synagogues were destroyed and many of his friends and neighbours disappeared. He was one of the lucky ones to escape to England on the Kindertransport scheme, and later to be re-united with his mother, but many members of his extended family were not so lucky.*

Rolf Heymann

I was born in 1928 in the village of Karpen near Cologne. My parents were Philip and Herta Heymann and our family was Jewish. I did not find out until much later that my father had been a hero and had won the Iron Cross in World War One. This was to have significant implications later in my life.

In 1930 my mother opened a sweetshop and library in the village. From the age of five onwards I became aware that Jewish boys were different from Christian boys, because I started getting beatings from members of the

Hitler Youth Movement. I knew that in some way or other Jews were not liked, but did not know why until I spoke to my mother and she explained. In 1937 my father died from the wound he had received in the First World War. In a way it was fortunate, as he did not have to suffer what we went through, or see our house smashed up, but it increased the responsibility of my mother.

Kristallnacht (Night of the Broken Glass) – the November Pogrom

I was eight-years-old on 10th November 1938, and the next day was to be my ninth birthday, which we were looking forward to, but in our village we knew that something was going to happen because we had a warning from one of our neighbours. The Christian family at the Smithy next door were very good friends of ours, and the man came to warn my mother that there would be trouble that night in all the Jewish houses. He said "Go into the house, put up the shutters to all the windows and hide in the cellar".

When he had gone, my mother told me we would have to go in the cellar for the night. She locked all the shutters and went into the cellar with me and my Aunty. Nothing happened at first and I must have fallen asleep. It was some time during the night when all of a sudden, we heard this terrible noise of the shattering of wood and smashing of glass. Despite the shutters an axe came smashing through and the noise was just terrible. Although they did not break into the house, every window and shutter had been broken.

The thing I remember is that I was so frightened. I honestly thought they were going to come into the house and kill us. I was only eight years old and was absolutely terrified. In fact, I have never been so frightened in my life before or since. There in the darkness of that cellar, the fear was just incredible, to the extent that I defecated into my trousers.

I will always remember the next day, my ninth birthday, when my mother took me to school. The local synagogue, with the school built on the side of it, had been burnt to the ground, and there was no school left. They had thrown all the Hebrew scrolls into the street. As a little lad I could hardly believe what I saw, it was so terrible. Our synagogue was just one of 101 destroyed that night, together with almost 7,500 Jewish businesses.

We came away from the synagogue and went to look for our Jewish friends and neighbours, going from house to house, but every door was open and the people gone. All of my school friends had disappeared and I never saw them again. I had to go to school in Cologne after that. Only one other Jewish family was left, so out of 133 Jewish people in the village, only six of us remained. They must have gone to the concentration camps.

I found out afterwards that only those six of us survived the War. The other family was a widow with two sons whose father, like mine, had also won an Iron Cross in the First World War. I am proud of my father's bravery in the First World War, because it is my belief that the reason the Nazis spared our families was for what our two fathers had done for Germany. So I have to thank my father for my being here today. It was almost the Nazis being decent, which they sometimes were at first, but as the War progressed, it did not matter what you or your family had done - if you were Jewish it would not save you.

The local authorities told us to get out of Germany if we valued our lives, and to get out as soon as we could.

The Kindertransport – my escape to Britain

The Jewish underground and the churches were involved in the organisation of the Kindertransport, which was an attempt to get 10,000 mostly Jewish children out of Germany, Austria and Czechoslovakia and give them asylum in England. I was very lucky to get on this. When most of the parents waved goodbye to the children on their way to Britain, for most of them it was the last time that they would see them.

My mother and aunt took me to Cologne railway station and put me on the train that would take me directly to Rotterdam in the Netherlands. They said goodbye to me and I did not know if I would ever see my mother or aunt again, but I was very excited at the thought of going on a big ship to England. I think the train went to the Dutch border, where the Gestapo boarded the train to check if we were all kids, then they let us through. The only other thing I remember was getting on the ship at Rotterdam to Harwich in England.

Sheffield

When we got to Harwich, my cousin who had come to live in England in 1936 with my Auntie and Uncle, met me. They lived in the Embassy Court Flats on the bottom of Duke Street, Sheffield. He had managed to get out of Germany early and had a job at Jessops in the offices. I arrived with my little suitcase containing underclothes and a ten shilling note (50p). They were my only possessions. I settled in Duke Street at those flats, which have since been demolished. It was a very rough area, and I went to Park School, which was also a very rough school.

I was only there a couple of months, but the kids took to me because I was treated as an oddity. I did not get the beatings because I was Jewish, like I did in Germany. I could only speak German, and all I could say in English was 'yes' and 'no', and I sometimes said them in the wrong places. Fortunately there was a schoolteacher at Park School called Mr Fox, who could speak a little bit of German. I was also very fortunate that my mother and aunt had escaped from Germany and had come to England just two weeks before the war started on September 3rd 1939. I saw them for a short while before I was evacuated.

Evacuation

On Saturday 2nd September 1939, the day before war was declared, 250 kids from Park School, together with Mr. Fox, were evacuated to a little village called Farnsfield, about halfway between Mansfield and Newark-on-Trent. I was billeted together with two other boys in a farmhouse just outside Farnsfield. On the first night the three of us went up the stairs to a very large room and slept the night in a large bed.

The next morning, as soon as we woke up, we went down the stairs into a massive kitchen where a maid was cooking Sunday breakfast. I had been brought up very strictly in the Jewish religion, and I mean very strict, and the thing that worried me most was that here were certain things I knew I should not eat. I smelt what she was cooking and it was a smell I had never smelt before. I asked her in German "What are you cooking?" but she could not understand me, but I kept on and eventually she realised what I wanted to know. She took me by the hand into the farmyard and showed me some pigs. When I realised she was cooking bacon, I actually heaved, because I knew I must not eat it, even though I had not eaten anything since four or five o'clock the previous day. My religious upbringing in Germany had been so strict that even the thought of pig would make me sick. I was heaving all morning and could not eat breakfast, not even the egg that had been cooked in the same pan as the bacon. I just had some dry bread.

Every morning, except weekends, it was to be a two-mile walk to school, and of course, a two-mile walk back. I picked up English quite easily because as I recall, there were only 150 children altogether at the Church of England school. There was no Jewish school or anything like it at Farnsfield, and if English is all you hear all day, and you do not hear any German, then you have got to listen and you have got to learn. I think that I learned

English well within six months. The family at the farm where I was billeted were Protestant. The lady wrote to my mother to say she thought I should have some religious upbringing and could she take me to church. The thought of her little Jewish boy going to a Christian church upset my mother very much and she said "No way", though I knew the lady at the farm had acted with the best of intentions.

My Family in Wartime Germany

I have two cousins who are twins, Inge and Ludwig. The Nazis sent them to Auschwitz Concentration Camp. There Dr Joseph Mengele, commonly referred to as the 'Angel of Death', had a special interest in twins. Being a twin, regardless of age, meant survival in 1944. He had selected 1,500 pairs of twins for experimentation. Of the children involved in these experiments, only 200 were alive when the Soviet army liberated the camp on January 27th 1945, and these included both of my cousins. They had survived only because Joseph Mengele had experimented on them. He had destroyed Inge's ovaries and he had sterilised Ludwig, but they were still alive. The twins are only a year older than me. They travelled to the U.S.A. and still write to me, but from what they say, they have not had a very happy life because of what happened to them in the camp.

Altogether just under 40 of my relatives perished.

Postscript

My mother was very,very grateful to the people of Britain for allowing us to settle in England. She used to express this gratitude in an unusual way. She used to write to Winston Churchill thanking him for letting us come to England, because she thought it was he who had allowed us to settle here. Every year on Churchill's birthday she would send him a card congratulating him on his birthday, and every year we would get a letter back from him, from 10 Downing Street, Whitehall, written in his own handwriting, thanking my mother for her good wishes. An example is: 'I am so much obliged to you for your kind token of good luck on my birthday. Winston S. Churchill'. My mother received two or three letters like that, and I was always in favour of her correspondence with Winston Churchill.

After Farnsfield I came back to Sheffield, left school at 14, and had many jobs, because I could not settle. As I grew up I acquired an inferiority complex that stayed with me until I married my wife, a local non-Jewish girl, whose parents were wonderful to me.

Every year I go back to Germany to visit my father's grave. When I go back there I never speak to any German over the age of 70. The other Germans, especially the young ones, feel really embarrassed. I get on with all Germans except those over 70 years of age because I think they could have been in the Nazi Party or the Hitler Youth.

Steven Mendelsson *lived in Poland, and also came to Britain before the War on the Kindertransport. He describes the bewilderment as he strove to adapt to life in a strange land, and to learn the language. More* *unsettling moves followed, due to evacuation, but there were also happy times, and some opportunities to contribute to the war effort on behalf of the country which had given him refuge.*

Steven Mendelsson

I was born in 1926 into a Jewish family in the city of Breslau in Germany (it is now called Wroclaw and is in Poland). My brother Walter was born in 1930 and we were a very happy family. Mother played the piano and Dad the violin and I played drums. I went to primary school where I was very happy and had lots of non-Jewish friends. We were an elite group of eight young lads (no girls allowed), who did lots of scrumping after school and kept our booty in a secret hiding place. Each day after school someone would be declared 'king of apples', or 'king of pears' based on how many we had stolen – we were never caught.

In Germany in those days birthdays were big events. Thus I attended seven fantastic parties in my friends' homes and of course, they all came to my birthday party. I was one of a group of eight very close friends and was the only Jew. In 1936 I went back to school after the summer holidays and suddenly realised that none of my mates would speak to me. I challenged one lad: "Fritz, why don't you talk to me?" He replied: "My father told me I mustn't talk to Jewish children". It was a real blow to my prestige. To be ignored is worse than being bullied, especially when it's your very best friends.

By a stroke of luck, within a few weeks, Hitler decreed that Jewish children were not allowed into schools, and at first we thought this was terrific – we were free: no teachers, rules, exams. However, soon after we gained this incredible freedom, we began to realise, quite independently, that we'd grow up and need a job and without schooling no one would employ us. In our city there were lots of Jewish teachers and lecturers who had lost their jobs, so they established a school specifically for Jewish children, which was allowed. That was fine for the first three weeks, until a local school half a mile away got to know about us. Every day as we left school the Hitler Youth from that school came to greet us and beat us up, three or four boys to one of us. Sometimes we were so badly hurt that we couldn't go to school next day. Presumably the Hitler Youth had some sort of code of honour, because they never beat up Jewish girls.

In November 1938 came Kristallnacht, when all the Jewish shops and synagogues were destroyed and all men between the ages of 16 and 65 were taken away to concentration camps. There were only three camps in Germany in those days, Dachau, Sachsenhausen and Buchenwald. My father was in the latter.

The world was appalled by this, and objected in strong terms, but the only country which did anything practical was Britain. After only one day's debate, the House of Commons, quickly followed by the Lords, voted to bring thousands of Jewish children here. This was discussed in November and the first trainload of children arrived at Liverpool Street station two days before Christmas.

The winter of 1938-9 was very severe, and in March 1939 my mother got a letter from the House of Commons in London, offering places for her two sons on the Kindertransport. She was to reply within 48 hours. Meanwhile, my father had been freed from Buchenwald just a few days earlier because Goering had decreed that all Jews who had fought for Germany in the First World War should be released. He was in such a hell of a state, malnourished, beaten up and had lost several toes with frostbite, that my mother forbade us to see him at first. The Nazis would not allow Jews to go into any of the German hospitals but there were plenty of Jewish doctors and nurses out of work and they helped my mother to treat him and nurse him back to reasonable health.

My mother, a courageous and God-fearing woman, said: "Let the children go, no matter what happens to us". Soon after, 20 children assembled at the railway station, with lots of parents, grandparents and other friends and relatives to see us off, with tears running down their faces. They cried so much they were hardly recognisable, but we kids were excited. We'd never been on such a long train journey before, right across North Germany and Holland, and then by boat to England, which we believed was the Garden of Eden.

As we set off, I remember how happy my brother and I were, and how sad were our parents. We were only allowed to take one suitcase filled with clothing, which we must be able to carry ourselves. The result was that we wore several layers of clothes. Wally and I had on two sets of underclothes, two shirts, one sweater, a jacket and overcoat, so we had these huge bodies with small heads and spindly legs.

We spent two days and two nights on the train until we reached the Hook of Holland and from there by ferry to Harwich. We were met by a reception committee of charming English ladies who hugged and kissed us but we were desperately tired, hot and thirsty. In Germany we would have been given a nice cold drink and some juicy fruit, but instead we got cups of hot tea, which we couldn't drink, and bananas which stuck in our dry throats.

Then we boarded a train to take us to Liverpool Street station in London. The train was old and only had wooden seats. We were amazed, because German trains were so modern and comfy. As we neared our destination, the train went through the East End of London, where we could see on either side houses with the roofs caved in and boarded up properties. We were shocked and frightened - this was the place we'd thought of as the Garden of Eden. Suddenly, we needed our parents to comfort us. For the first time we realised that we were high and dry, totally alone in an antiquated train in a strange country whose language we could not speak, with food we couldn't eat. It was a grim shock – we were orphans.

Liverpool Street station was as antiquated as the train. We were taken to a hall, about 250 of us, and in rushed lots of charming English couples prepared to take in

Jewish children. It was like a cattle market: "turn round, lift your arm, your leg". Most people wanted girls and Wally and I were two very normal little boys. Ultimately we were picked by a couple who drove us off to Maida Vale in their car. Very few people had cars in those days and I felt like the King being driven through London in his Rolls Royce.

We stayed there one week and then went to a hostel in Margate for boys, being run by a Jewish relief organisation. There were 60 boys in the hostel and soon we were to be integrated into English schools. Few of us spoke English – we had learnt Latin and French in Germany, so there was a seminar held in the hostel to teach us the basics. This lasted half an hour and when we could say "please" and "thank you" we were sent out to local schools, where not a single child could speak German. So, how to communicate? One of us, at 14, was a brilliant thinker. He figured that here we were in an English school, with English kids, we must learn the language – and we accepted his theory. Those kids were lovely – they taught us all the swear words and dirty words they knew, and of course, we didn't know what they meant and spoke them to the teachers! The teachers were great and soon put us right. Within six months we were speaking English and into football and even that most ridiculous game – cricket. We were integrated!

The War began in September 1939, and my parents came here 36 hours before war was declared, on the last transport from France. They remained in London throughout the War and were bombed out three times. In Margate we were in the front line. When the army was evacuated from Dunkirk, we were asked to volunteer to help with the returning troops. I was with a nurse, and my job at 13, was to light a cigarette (a Woodbine) and put it into the lips of every soldier. I probably lit a thousand cigarettes in three days and because they were not tipped cigarettes my lips swelled as a result, beyond any recognition.

Very soon after Dunkirk, our school was evacuated to South Staffordshire and we were billeted with miners' families. The first billet Wally and I had was very unpleasant, but my constant attempts to get it changed all failed. At 14 I was promoted to prefect and then senior prefect, my main function being to cane late-comers. By this means I had gained recognition and the Billeting Officer told me of two other possibilities and I rode off on my bike to see them.

The first one I saw was the home of a miner, but they kept free-range chickens and two pigs, guarded by two lovely Collie dogs. We took to them like a duck to water and they to us. They were the most wonderful people and I am still in touch with the family to this day. At first, the locals couldn't understand that while they were fighting a war against the Germans, they were asked by the Government to care for German children. We were, of course, by nationality German, but Jewish refugees from Nazi persecution, and we were even more eager than they for Britain to win the War. It took almost six weeks for them to realise we were okay. I have never lived in so humane a community, both towards themselves and the outside world. We had a wonderful time.

At 14 I left school and went out to work, getting an apprenticeship with an engineering company which made precision tools. My education at school had been pathetic. The teachers were all third rate because the proper ones had been called up into the Services. I was expected to teach classes in P.E. and gardening. The family we stayed with had a son called Alan the same age as Wally (10) and he passed a scholarship and went to Grammar School.

I felt that I was responsible for my younger brother, so I encouraged him to swot with Alan, with a view to him obtaining a scholarship. I got a letter addressed to “The Father of Walter”, saying that my brother had passed the entrance exam but “we can’t offer him a place because he is not Staffordshire-born”. When I told the Head we were refugees from Nazi oppression, he rethought his decision and with a broad smile said: “Your brother is in – good luck to you”. So Wally at least had a good education, but I didn’t.

During my apprenticeship, which involved working 12-hour shifts, two weeks on days and two weeks on nights, I asked the boss if I could go to Night School. He was very understanding and gave me time off three nights a week. I went to the local Technical/Commercial College so as to pass the Matriculation and get into a university.

I had been very keen to join the RAF, having been in the Air Training Corps for two years in the pilot/navigator group. They suddenly found from my initial entry documents that I was a German National. Regretfully they dismissed me there and then. My teacher at Night School was a Scotsman and a Captain of the Home Guard, so he arranged for me to join. This Home Guard was not a bit like Dad's Army because Walsall was an industrial area, so there were lots of fit men who were in reserved occupations, and who belonged to the Home Guard.

We were on the outskirts of Birmingham which was surrounded by anti-aircraft barrages and Walsall had eight of these anti-aircraft guns manned solely by the Home Guard and ATS girls. I had an interview with the C.O. and on the first day he took me to the gun emplacements, introduced me and showed me all the installations. He told me: "You and I are the only ones in the battalion who know the location of the gun emplacements". Security was ridiculous!

I was 19 when the War ended. I reckon that Wally and I were among less than 10 per cent of the 10,000 or so children that Britain saved from the Nazi clutches, who were re-united with their parents. All the other children's parents, as well as our entire extended family, were victims of the Holocaust.

Britain was the only country that courageously and humanely gave these 10,000 children the chance to survive and to progress. We always remain exceedingly grateful. Today I am an old codger enjoying life, albeit with many senior moments, still as much in love with my wife. I have three wonderful children with their spouses, and three delightful grandchildren.

***Otto Jakubovic** has a darker tale to tell. There was no escape for him from occupied Czechoslovakia, and he spent his teenage years in Ghettos and Concentration Camps. He was one of the few who survived, against tremendous odds.*

Dr Otto Jakubovic

In 1939 I was 11-years-old and living in Prague, Czechoslovakia with my father, my parents having divorced when I was very young and my mother having re-married. Hitler invaded Czechoslovakia in March 1939, but my father was a G.P. and late in 1938 had been mobilised in the Army Medical Corps as a captain. To escape the Nazis, he fled the country. He had to go alone if he was to succeed, but from then on he tried to get me out to join him.

I didn't even know he was going to England, and was now virtually an orphan. A kind Protestant lady, Mrs Slechtova, one of his grateful patients, took me into her home and looked after me. She lived in a small spa town 20 miles from Prague. Her husband was an inspector of railways and had free family travel, which included me, so I could commute into Prague to my old school. However, very soon after the German occupation Jewish children were restricted in schooling, as other things.

From the summer of 1940 I could not continue in my Czech real gymnasium (secondary or grammar school), so I was virtually confined to the property of the lady looking after me. As it had a nice garden with apple trees, paddling pool and an Alsatian dog which was my best friend, I was not unhappy. Not only was I forbidden to go to school, but soon the local German governor, an SA Officer, pronounced that our town was to be Juden Frei (a Jew-free area). He threatened my guardian family that if they didn't get rid of me they could go to prison.

After much soul-searching they applied to the Jewish orphanage in Prague and at 13 years of age, I went there. Now I could go out and about, but only if wearing the yellow Star of David. It was not pleasant, as if a German came by I had to get off the pavement and would often get a kick in the backside. The orphanage provided a modicum of education. Life went on till in September 1942 it became apparent that Jews were being taken away, and so I was transported to the Ghetto at Terezin near the German border.

There were 59,000 internees. It was originally a fortress town designed for 15,000 troops, built by the Empress Maria Theresa in order to protect the Hapsburg Empire from the Swedes. It was a walled town, with huge barrack blocks four storeys high. Due to its size and compactness it was chosen as the Jewish Ghetto. The Germans forcibly emptied the town of the Czechs who lived there and closed it off. It was a bit of luck for me that I was an orphan, so I was not housed in the big barracks with families, but in a Boys' Home. It had nine or ten rooms each holding 30 boys, graded by age, with bunks three tiers high.

Although under surveillance the whole time, the Ghetto was administered by a Jewish Community Leader and a Council of Elders who wanted to keep life as normal as possible for us. We must be surreptitiously educated, and there was no lack of teachers, including academics from the universities. They weren't used to teaching children, but did their best. We could also go out into the fields and do some agricultural work which enabled us to pinch the odd potato and other vegetables and bring them back to eat. The Council tried to ensure we had games to play, even football matches were organised and several Youth Leaders were based with us and looked after us. The leader in my room was a good tennis player. He survived the War and returned to Czechoslovakia, becoming a tennis coach, even coaching the team, one of whom won Wimbledon post-war.

We were isolated from the harshest things and we were not starving. We could also receive Red Cross parcels. As my mother had married a Catholic and had converted to that faith, she was protected, at least during the early years, and sent me parcels from time to time. Some of these contained delicacies which I treasured and put aside for harder times, but in the end, I never got to eat them. I had jaundice, and was quite seriously ill, being too unwell to perform in a children's opera. Many others caught typhus and it is estimated that 40,000 died of it.

Rumours began to circulate that we were destined for transport East, and periodically 1,000 or more would be put on trains. We knew that one thing to avoid was going East. The Germans even built a spur of the railway into the Ghetto so no one ever went outside. This continued into 1943, and many of my friends were included. My turn came on 18th May when 2,500 of us were loaded into cattle trucks and sent to Auschwitz. One reason our departure was so rapid was that the Germans had invited the Red Cross to inspect Terezin to show how nice it was. They cleaned it up, set up orchestras etc and completely fooled the Red Cross. Out of the 150,000 people who passed through Terezin, almost 15,000 were children, of whom only about 100 survived the War.

Our arrival at Auschwitz was one of the unforgettable moments of my life. We stopped at a railway junction, the doors slid open and at that moment were assailed by an unforgettable smell of tremendous intensity, which can only be appreciated by those who were there. It was the smell of burning human flesh. The area was surrounded by electric barbed wire fences and I could see the smoke and flames of the crematoria chimneys.

The SS guards, with their hounds and stick, demanded all of our possessions and I lost the jar of apricot preserve I had been saving for the future. It is a fact that you cannot survive in these kind of situations without a modicum of luck. My first stroke of luck took place here. I hung back a little and noticed lines being marched up in front of an SS man (this was Dr Mengele), who would give either a thumbs left or right sign to each person. They would then go separate ways. I could see that the fit ones, who were neither too young nor too old, got the thumb sign one way, so when it was my turn to stand in front of him and give my age and occupation, I made myself older and instead of 16, said I was 18. I did not say I was a schoolboy, but rather a gardener, as this would imply I was able to do hard physical work. I got the thumb sign the right way!

All the people who got the other sign went immediately to the gas chambers. I went through Reception, had my camp number tattooed on, my clothes taken away and was given wooden clogs, then allocated to buildings. There were 300 or 400 in our hut, in bunks three storeys high and wide enough to take six people in a tight squeeze. We could not turn over in bed without disturbing the others. There were no toilets or water supply in the hut. My camp was Auschwitz-Birkenau B2B. We were all Czech Jews, but the whole of the Auschwitz concentration camp complex contained some 100,000 internees.

To some extent I had made my own luck the first time, but over the second I had no influence. It came about as a result of D-Day 6th June 1944. The normal lifespan of prisoners in Birkenau was six months, after which they automatically went to the gas chambers, but now the Germans needed labour, and we were a large pool of potential forced labour. On 1st July Mengele selected 1,000 inmates who looked fit, and I was among them. I was on the first transport in cattle trucks to Germany early in July. We travelled to central Germany north of Dresden, where a big factory produced petrol products for the war effort. Our camp, Schwarzheide (a sub-camp of Sachsenhausen concentration camp), was on one side of the big Autobahn between Berlin and Dresden, and on the other side was the factory.

Again, my luck was in. Being the youngest in the group and the only one clean-shaven, I was chosen by the SS officer in charge to become his Leufer i.e. runner, to run his errands and take messages etc. This meant that I sat on a stool near a bell, and when it rang I ran across to the officers' quarters, stood to attention and received my orders. This was a huge privilege, as all the others went to work in the factory. They worked there till April 1945 and many of them died, because in the winter they had no warm clothing, no shoes except clogs, and walking to and from the factory each day amounted to a death sentence in the long, freezing cold winter. Meanwhile I was in a fairly warm place and had occasional access to extra soup. The downside was that the SS officer gave me frequent beatings with a horsewhip, one of which was so severe that I fainted and had to be carried into the camp.

The allies bombed the factory, though many bombs fell on an artificial fire which had been lit elsewhere to draw them from the main target, and one bomb strayed into the camp. There was also a fogging plant which created artificial fog to cover areas they wanted to protect, but a bomb hit that and dispersed the fog, so that the next wave of bombers hit the target and crippled the factory.

This was in March 1945. Our job was to replace piping and mend roadways, but the factory was now of no use and by then the Russians were advancing and the War drawing to a close.

Hitler decided that the Autobahn would be the last line of defence. No one was to be allowed to go West, but again luck intervened. The guards had been ordered to kill all unreliable elements and defend the frontier, but they decided to march us away instead. This was the start of the death marches. One thousand of us set off in mid-to-late April, and we walked in our 'striped pyjamas' and wooden clogs from dawn to dusk, spending the nights in fields or barns, surrounded by guards. The guards had transport, trucks, motor bikes etc, but we walked. There was no food, we picked up bits of carrot and potato by the roadside, though we were not allowed to stop. If someone collapsed they were put in a ditch and shot, so we made a rule that we'd support anyone who collapsed for one day, to give them chance to recover overnight, but we couldn't do so forever. After two and a half to three weeks, only 256 of the thousand were left, and this was now the point of liberation.

We were marching towards the Czech border. One night we collapsed to rest after a long march, and the next morning when we woke up, the guards had gone. Within hours Russian army lorries came by en route to Germany and they threw bread and chocolates to us. Soon after that, the Czech Red Cross vans came and guided us to the nearest village, which was actually quite near to Terezin. We were deloused, cleaned up and given clothes and international passes which were in four languages: Russian, English, French and Czech. The pass said that this person should be given every help.

In Terezin I bumped into my mother, who had been transported even whilst the fighting at the end of the War was going on. She had arrived a few weeks prior to me. I was very underweight, just skin and bone. We were examined, treated, and as soon as possible I went to see the lady who had been my guardian, Mrs Slechtova, in the little town outside Prague. My pass got me help and I was able to hitch–hike on a lorry and then take a train to Prague. When I knocked at her door, my former guardian nearly fainted – she could not believe that I had survived and was delighted. Her eldest son had gone to Prague to help in the fighting and she couldn't stop me joining him.

It was 8th May 1945, VE Day in England, and the peace treaty had been signed.

After spending a few weeks in a Czech convalescent home, I located my father through a refugee organisation which broadcast appeals for contacts of refugees with family members who had escaped overseas before the War. He was in Manchester. I was then flown out from Prague airport with 300 other children in stripped-out RAF Lancaster bombers. We landed at an RAF base in the Lake District called Crosby-in-Eden. From there my father collected me, and I began my post war life.

"We were the Enemy"

In these two stories of children growing up in Italy and Austria, it is striking how similar are some of their experiences to those of children in Britain. The disruptions, privations and sorrows of wartime life are seen to be much the same, no matter what side you are on.

Luisella Chatwin's *father served in the Italian Army on the Russian Front. She and her mother moved from Turin to safety in the country, and when they did return to the city towards the end of the War, they found themselves in the midst of fighting between Mussolini's supporters and the anti-fascist partisans, whilst the allied armies advanced northwards.*

Luisella Chatwin

I was born in Turin in December 1938. My father was a solicitor, my mother was French, and I had one sister four years older than me. In March 1941 my father was conscripted into the Army. A photograph of his unit on parade shows one of Mussolini's slogans on a wall behind. It reads "The laugh and happiness of young children, the strength of the youth, the energy of maturity". These slogans got left on the walls and some could still be seen for years after the War ended.

In a photograph of my mother, sister and I standing in the street at some event with soldiers behind us my sister, about five-years-old, is wearing a rosette to show support for Mussolini and the Fascists. You had to do this whether you supported them or not. The Fascists were against the Jews. My grandma had a Jewish friend whose daughter was hidden by nuns. She said that if she came out alive and free, and lived to have children, she would become a Catholic, and so she did.

Some of the Italian army were sent to Africa and some to Russia. Very few came back from Africa so my father was lucky to be sent to Russia where they were treated quite well by the populace. He was wounded in 1944, just before the big retreat, and though he lost a large number of his men, he returned to us and was able to go back to a desk job in the Army.

My mother must have found the War very difficult as she was French and was cut off from all her family by the German occupation. However, she had a friend (also French) whose husband had contacts in Switzerland through his work and so got information occasionally through those channels.

My mother's sister, Georgette, was a Red Cross nurse in Marseilles and was involved in the evacuation of French children to North Africa. She would accompany them on the boat going over and also brought them back at the end of the War. Sadly the boat they travelled on was very old and unsafe and it sank. She and all the children were drowned. She was only 28-years-old. My mother's younger sister was married to a man who was in the Free French Airforce with General de Gaulle. He was shot down and killed without ever knowing his daughter.

While my father was away we moved to Limoné, a little town in the mountains of Piedmont, near the Italian/French border. The local people were not too keen at having us townies there, but on the whole my life was happy and carefree. We had quite good food from the local farmers which we obtained on a bartering system, exchanging children's clothing for milk and eggs. I went to a nursery school run by nuns who were very strict. They told us that make-up was sinful and should all be thrown away so I went home and threw my mother's lipstick down the toilet. She was not pleased as cosmetics were hard to get. Another time the priest preached a sermon saying that the knitting my mother and other townswomen were doing on Sundays was sinful, as it was breaking the Sabbath Day.

I didn't know anything about my father while he was absent but suddenly he reappeared. One day my mother left us with friends and came back with Father. He had been hurt by a bomb blast and rendered deaf. It was peaceful in the mountains and we didn't really know that a war was going on.

In 1944-5 we returned to Turin. Our flats were located between three barracks so we heard the sound of gunfire all the time. I was so frightened that I'd go up and down the stairs screaming. Once we had a young man staying with us. He was the son of my mother's friend, a Partisan who had to hide. We were told not to tell anyone that we had a guest – it was a big secret. He stayed three or four months and then went away.

Bread was the only food in short supply. I recall queuing for bread but not other foods. In the middle of queuing the sirens would go and we'd run away – this was quite exciting to me as a child. Often we couldn't get bread at all. One of my Dad's soldiers was a butcher in a country town so my dad bought a pig called 'Benito' and the man butchered it for us. He was loyal and close to my father. We didn't have sweets, but American soldiers gave us chocolates and we had little parties for our birthdays.

The end of the War was the worst time for Italy, because there was a lot of fighting between the Partisans and the Fascists. The American and British armies landed in Sicily and advanced North, but there were still many fascists fighting.

At one point Mussolini escaped from Rome to a town called Salo on Lake Garda where he created a new and short-lived Republica da Salo. As we were so near the Swiss border many of his supporters escaped into Switzerland. They were hanging people in the streets and it was quite dangerous to go out walking. Women who had collaborated with the Germans had all their hair cut off. One woman (who had gone out with a German officer) had this happen to her and she disappeared for a while till her hair grew back.

By 1946 things were quieter. My brother was born that year and my mother resumed communication with her family in France.

***Dorothy Thompson's** war began earlier than ours, when her pleasant family life was torn apart by the murder of her father during a Nazi uprising in 1934, followed by the Anschluss (German Occupation) in 1938. From that time on, the various family members took very different stances, while Dorothy's widowed mother tried to maintain home-life amidst food shortages, air raids and all the other disruptions which war brings about.*

Dorothy Thompson

I was born Dorothea Wolf, in 1931, in the small lakeside village of Steindorf in Austria, which is near the town of Villach and close to the border with Italy. I was the fourth of five children. My father was a policeman and also kept a smallholding. Half of our home was a stable for the animals and we lived in the other half.

In 1934 there was a small Nazi uprising in the next village and my father went to see what was happening. He hid behind the stooks of corn in a field, but was found and shot dead. My eldest brother Franz, then 17-years-old, had followed my father and saw what happened from his hiding place. My mother was 6 months pregnant at the time, and I remember I had to wear a black dress with white ribbons. A stone memorial to my father was erected at the place where he was shot, and is still there to this day. After my father's death my mother gave up the smallholding, and because he had been a policeman, she was able to get a mortgage and buy a large house up the hillside, but we were quite poor. All of us, no matter how young, had jobs to do about the house.

In 1938 the Germans put on pressure for our two countries to unite. Our Chancellor wanted to hold a referendum and was pretty sure the answer would be "No" but the Austrian Nazi Party organised a coup d'etat. German soldiers entered Austria to enforce the union, known as the Anschluss and a plebiscite was held about this closer link with Germany. Everyone had to vote, and had to wear little metal badges with swastikas on. My mother was scared stiff because so many officials at the polling station were members of the Nazi Party. They wore their badges under their lapels until the elections were won. Some people, like her, were loyal Austrians and did not want the Germans. Perhaps 70% of the population were against it, but mentally some were already attached to the Nazi party, and the 'results' were said to be 99% for the union.

I was eight or nine years old when the War broke out, and my mother cried her eyes out. She had lived through the First World War and lost all her savings, and now she would lose everything again. Our village was never bombed but the nearby big town was, and this is where we went to school. We travelled by train but there was only one per day each way (and no school dinners). I grew up with the idea of sharing – you shared what you had. I would save some of my bread and butter lunch to share with others on the train home. When there was an air-raid, which was usually about 11 am, the Headmaster would come and tell us to go home, which meant a walk of ten miles, so our education was greatly disrupted.

At school we were indoctrinated against the Jews, but to me they were just people. The cattle trucks taking them away to the concentration camps would go through the railway at our village and we were so sorry for them. They would be crammed in with no food or water for maybe days, and our village Stationmaster could see some of them looking through the iron grilles in the trucks. He used to direct the water from the overhead channels used to fill up the steam engines, so that it ran onto and down the wagons. That way at least some of them got a drink.

Living in a police state, we had to tow the line. Members of your own family could inform against you and you'd disappear. Two boys I went to school with suddenly disappeared. When I asked my mother what happened to them, she said that the family were Jehovah's Witnesses, which was forbidden, and they went to Dachau concentration camp.

We learnt at an early age not to think it a sin to buy off the black market, and we would trade for food, perhaps one saccharin tablet for a little sweetness. I used to help the old lady who ran the village shop and she would sometimes give me an eggcupful of sugar as a treat. Even so, my mother usually managed to get us some sweet biscuits at Christmas and Easter. We helped at a farm and got a lovely lunch, which helped my mother. Mother also kept some chickens, rabbits and a pig. She hated having to kill the chickens and would be upset and angry for a few days afterwards, so we'd try to keep out of her way.

We listened to the news. My mother, who didn't like being told what to do, listened to the Swiss radio, which was forbidden, but she got proper news, not just propaganda. My sisters were of the same mind as our mother and I too wanted to support her. One of my sisters, Eva, and the son of the old lady at the village shop, used to listen to the news on a secret radio in the attic. If found out, they could have gone to a concentration camp. Towards the end of the War when the Germans were being beaten on all fronts the Gauleiter would visit the families of soldiers and tell them they had been killed, but my sister found out from the radio this was not true and so she sent postcards to the families to say: "Your son or husband is alive".

My oldest brother was a student in the big town and lodged with a family there, who had two boys. All three of them joined the SS, which was an elite force. They were idealistic and full of bravado, but the other two dropped out when the training became tough. My brother, who had joined in secret because he knew our mother would not approve, was too proud to give up – he couldn't admit that he had made a mistake.

He fought through the whole War, initially based at Calais awaiting the invasion of England. Then he was sent to the Russian Front, to Latvia, where he was attacked by partisans and left half dead. However, he recovered, and when the War ended he walked homewards. At Schleswig he was caught by Russian troops, but they let him go, and he reached Munich. There the Americans caught him and he spent two years in a prisoner of war camp in France where he was very badly treated. I used to help a neighbouring farmer who would give me lunch – sausage, bread and apple. I would save it up and we'd send it to my brother in the French camp. His little boy was six years old when he came home and had never seen him before. His wife had saved and bartered in order to get him some shoes and clothing and he took a job as a forester.

My sister Linda was in the Land Army and was stationed at a camp in Yugoslavia. Half the Yugoslavs were partisans, fighting the Germans, and my sister joined them but she was captured and sent to a prison at Marburg, where she was badly beaten. When the War ended she walked home – her face was so swollen, my mother was heartbroken.

There were two English prisoner of war camps in the village and they were well provided with Red Cross parcels. We'd see the postman's cart full of them – and that really impressed us with the English. Another thing that impressed us was that when the RAF came bombing and strafing the railway line, they always criss-crossed the line first, to enable the people in the train to get away, then they would bomb it. Although the English were 'the enemy' we always thought of them as a highly civilised nation.

The farmers' wives did washing for the POWs, who 'paid' them by trading goods from their Red Cross parcels, maybe soap and chocolate. Some prisoners worked on the railway and once they were deprived of water for 48 hours, due to a British air raid. Money was worth nothing and the POWs had none, so trading was the way they paid. One of the English prisoners escaped and was sheltered for a month at the house of a prostitute – he was not caught, but I never found out whether he got back to England.

We never went to the cellar during the bombing. As our house was so high up, we could see the bombers below us sometimes, diving along the railway. Sometimes they jettisoned their petrol tanks and the local farmers would collect them, as petrol was scarce.

About three weeks before the end of the War, we knew the British were coming up from Italy, and the Russians from Yugoslavia, and we were all praying the British would get there first, which they did. Thousands of soldiers, lorries and armoured cars came along the road. They requisitioned nice houses for accommodation for the soldiers, and my future husband, Bob, was billeted at our house. He'd been one of the first to enter Austria, with a Pathe News camera on the back of the lorry.

My mother knew Bob was the one who had whistled at me from the road. He was so sunburnt from Italy that her first words were: "My God, he's a Negro!" I was sixteen but he was the one for me. He was demobbed in 1947 and asked me to marry him. I needed lots of documents and permissions to come to England and had to be married within two weeks or I'd be sent home. Bob had to go to a Commissioner of Oaths and swear that he would be responsible for me. I arrived with two suitcases and no money – he took me just as I was.

First I stayed with friends of his in London and Bob bought me a lovely pair of brown shoes, as I only had one pair. I wore them for years. His cousin lent me my wedding outfit. I came to a lovely, decent English family in Rotherham, who took me in without question. Never once did I feel animosity from anyone - most normal people don't want war – they just want to look after each other. We were the enemy but we just saw ourselves as people immersed in war. Bob called me his war booty.